P9-CES-242

PRAISE FOR *DO OVER*

"This is the best career book ever written. I'm not even sure what book comes in second. This is practical, human, touching, urgent, vulnerable, universal, actionable truth, all in a well-written, handy package. Go!"

—SETH GODIN, author of *What to Do When It's Your Turn*

"As Abraham Lincoln once said, being forced into work you don't love is like paying to upgrade your cell phone to the latest model: no one should have to do that! Fortunately, you don't need to do at least one of these things anymore. Take it from me and from Honest Abe: Jon's book can get you unstuck."

—CHRIS GUILLEBEAU, author of *The Happiness of Pursuit* and *The $100 Startup*

"*Do Over* is an energetic, user-friendly guide to navigating the jumps, bumps, and ceilings that we all face in our careers."

—ADAM GRANT, author of *Give and Take*

"Jon Acuff has redefined the entire category of career books. *Do Over* is so easy and fun to read, you almost forget how much you're learning. But the lessons he shares—lessons picked up the hard way and told with honesty and heart—will help anyone looking to keep moving forward in their career. This is career guidance in hyperdrive."

—BRIAN KOPPELMAN, screenwriter/filmmaker, *Rounders*, *Ocean's 13*, and *Solitary Man*

"Warning: Only read this book if you are prepared to completely revolutionize your career, your goals, your dreams, your plans, and basically your *life*. Jon takes a topic that tends to terrify the average human (including me)—starting over—and turns it into an exciting and life-changing adventure that makes even a person not looking for a do-over want a do-over. If you're stuck, frustrated in your career, lost a job, or feel like you're missing out on your dream while you help someone else chase theirs . . . this is the book for you."

—MANDY HALE, *New York Times* bestselling author of *I've Never Been to Vegas, but My Luggage Has* and creator of @TheSingleWoman

"This straightforward, hilarious, yet intensely practical book is your guide to career success in the new century. Jon Acuff tells you, from his hard-won experience, what you need to do to stay happily employed and highly employable. Free from complicated matrices and useless jargon, you will love the read almost as much as you love the advice."

—PAMELA SLIM, author of *Body of Work*

"*Do Over* is one of those rare gems that is not only packed with practical, hard-earned wisdom but is thoroughly enjoyable to read. Whether or not you are in a time of transition, Jon Acuff shows you how to prepare today for whatever is next."

—TODD HENRY, author of *Die Empty*

"Honest, funny, helpful, fresh: there's a long list of words to describe the wisdom you'll find in *Do Over*. I dare you to read the first few pages of this book. If you're like me, you won't be able to stop. I have ordered a copy for every member of my team."

—MICHAEL HYATT, author of *Platform*

"Big dreams often start with big books. *Do Over* is one of them. The impact this book is going to have on the careers and lives of people across the world is going to be really fun to watch!"

—ANDY ANDREWS, author of *The Noticer* and *The Traveler's Gift*

"Jon Acuff serves up heaping portions of sage advice with a healthy side of self-deprecating humor. As an entrepreneur and business owner, I found myself nodding, laughing, and getting my toes stepped all over in a good way throughout these pages."

—CRYSTAL PAINE, founder of MoneySavingMom.com and author of *Say Goodbye to Survival Mode*

"If you're sick of constantly fighting the Monday blues, this book is for you. . . . [Acuff's] career advice is solid. . . . By the end, most will have a new outlook on their role in the workplace. They will be ready to take on the day with nothing but an adjusted attitude and a ton of grit."

—Associated Press

© Jeremy Cowart

PORTFOLIO / PENGUIN

DO OVER

JON ACUFF is the author of five books, including *Quitter* and the *New York Times* bestseller *Start*. For nineteen years he has helped companies like Home Depot, Bose, Staples, and AutoTrader.com tell their stories. He's a well-known public speaker, and his blogs have been read by millions of fans. He lives in Nashville with his wife, Jenny, and their two young daughters.

Follow Jon on Twitter @JonAcuff and on the web at www.Acuff.me.

Share your story on Twitter, Instagram, Pinterest, and Facebook with #DoOverBook.

DO OVER

Make Today the First Day of Your
New Career

JON ACUFF

PORTFOLIO / PENGUIN

PORTFOLIO / PENGUIN

An imprint of Penguin Random House LLC
375 Hudson Street
New York, New York 10014
penguin.com

First published in the United States of America by Portfolio / Penguin 2015
This paperback edition published 2017

Copyright © 2015 by Jonathan Acuff
Penguin supports copyright. Copyright fuels creativity, encourages diverse voices, promotes free speech, and creates a vibrant culture. Thank you for buying an authorized edition of this book and for complying with copyright laws by not reproducing, scanning, or distributing any part of it in any form without permission. You are supporting writers and allowing Penguin to continue to publish books for every reader.

Most Portfolio books are available at a discount when purchased in quantity for sales promotions or corporate use. Special editions, which include personalized covers, excerpts, and corporate imprints, can be created when purchased in large quantities. For more information, please call (212) 572-2232 or e-mail specialmarkets@penguinrandomhouse.com. Your local bookstore can also assist with discounted bulk purchases using the Penguin Random House corporate Business-to-Business program. For assistance in locating a participating retailer, e-mail B2B@penguinrandomhouse.com.

Illustrations by William C. Warren. Copyright © 2015 by Jonathan Acuff.

ISBN 9781591847618 (hc.)
ISBN 9780143109693 (pbk.)

Printed in the United States of America
10 9 8 7 6 5 4 3 2 1

Set in Adobe Garamond Pro
Designed by Jaime Putorti

While the author has made every effort to provide accurate telephone numbers, Internet addresses, and other contact information at the time of publication, neither the publisher nor the author assumes any responsibility for errors or for changes that occur after publication. Further, the publisher does not have any control over and does not assume any responsibility for author or third-party Web sites or their content.

For Jenny, of course.

Contents

1 The Career Savings Account 1

2 Do This First 21

INVESTMENT 1
RELATIONSHIPS

3 You Don't Know Who You Know 29

4 Give Your Foes What They Need Most 40

5 Casual Counts 53

6 Great Careers Take Great Advocates 63

7 Don't Burn Many Bridges 76

8 Community Shines Brightest
in the Darkness of a Career Bump 82

INVESTMENT 2
SKILLS

9 You Have More Skills Than You Think 93

10 Master the Invisible Skills 102

11 Never Become a Dinosaur 113

12 Win the Way You Won Before 120

13 Kick-Start Your New Skills with Something Fun 124

14 Skills Get Sharp Slowly and Dull Quickly   135
15 Grab the Right Kind of Hammer for Your Career Ceiling   145

INVESTMENT 3
CHARACTER

16 Plant an Orchard   157
17 Generosity Is a Game Changer   167
18 Empathy, No Longer Just for People
   Who Like to Cry with Friends   177
19 Be Present   193
20 Never Jump Without Character   202

INVESTMENT 4
HUSTLE

21 Grit Is a Choice, Not a Feeling   211
22 Hustle Has Seasons: Use Awareness to Recognize Them   227
23 Career Yoga   237
24 Always Use This to Multiply the Moment   253
25 Three Final Words You'll Tell Me Someday Soon   258
   Acknowledgments   263
   Notes   273

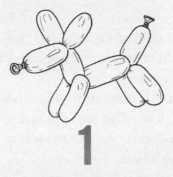

1

The Career Savings Account

When you're a mailman, you shouldn't ask people if you can use their bathroom.

In hindsight, I probably didn't need to learn that lesson via personal experience. And yet, there I stood on the front steps with today's mail and an awkward request.

As a creative writer, I made for a pretty horrible mailman. I was disorganized, fumbling and prone to get pepper spray in my own eyes. One day I switched my morning route with my afternoon route, which meant people who usually got the mail late got it early. A happy homeowner told me I was way better than that other guy, unknowingly referring to me. I agreed, telling her, "He's the worst. Just a real jerk."

My career arc would continue through places like "Apple Country," a convenience store that did not sell apples, and "Maurice the Pants Man," no Maurice but plenty of pants.

I'd spend sixteen years traveling through corporate America, writing advertising for the Home Depot, branding for Bose and marketing for Staples. I was laid off from one start-up, fired from another, ran my own into the ground and then found and left my dream job. Along the way, I learned one lesson about work.

You control more than you think.

Good job, bad job, dream job, no job, this is true.

It's on us. Though we often prefer to blame others or the economy or a boss who doesn't "get us," the reality is that a better job begins with building a better you.

Work is not the enemy.

Work does not have to be a miserable bar-free prison we voluntarily serve time in until the parole of retirement. On the contrary, work can be great.

Work can be wonderful.

If we rescue Monday. If we dare to reinvent it. If we refuse to get stuck.

This book isn't about quitting a job. (I already wrote that one, it's called *Quitter* because I'm creative like that.)

This book isn't about starting something. (I already wrote that one too; it's called *Start*.)

This book is about intentionally building a career using the four investments every extraordinary career has in common.

The investments are so obvious you just might miss them. The balloon animal guy certainly did with me that night in the field.

Lest you fear I spend the weirdest Craigslist-initiated weekends ever, let me back up a second. I assure you I can explain my moonlit rendezvous with the man in the rainbow suspenders.

I was waiting in line with my wife and kids at Family Fun Night at our local elementary school. It was Friday night and next to the face-painting lady, the balloon guy is whom you visit immediately at events like that.

While twisting and pulling at the colorful balloons, this craftsman of inflated rubber looked down at me from the stool he was standing on.

"I love your books," he said, recognizing me and smiling, but then some other thought dimmed his otherwise bright eyes.

"Sorry about today," he added in a more serious tone. "I wish you the best in your future endeavors."

The balloon animal guy was encouraging me because he believed I lost a lot.

And he was right, I did lose something. We always do when we leave old places for new adventures.

That morning, I left my dream job.

In the process, I left behind products, money and the craziest opportunities I'd ever had.

If you tallied the day, it might be my most loserish day of all time. Even reading about what I left behind made me feel a little like I was going to scream Phil Collins lyrics at the balloon animal guy: "Take a look at me now, oh there's just an empty space."

I don't blame the guy wearing a fanny pack of balloons for worrying about the future of my career.

But I had something he didn't know about.

A tool kit I would have never jumped without.

A tool kit you probably already have too.

A tool kit my friend Nate was about to need.

▪ The Day Everything Changed

My neighbor Nate lost his job on a Friday.

If you are ever invited to a late Friday afternoon meeting with your boss, that's not a meeting, that's a booby trap.

Nate's career quickly changed that day.

He was suddenly afloat and not by his own choice.

I met with him the next week for coffee.

With a dazed expression he told me how he felt losing a job he'd had for eight years.

He was good at it. He always hit his numbers. People liked him. Clients texted their condolences to him days after it had happened. He was and still is a great guy.

But he was in trouble.

Cocooned for eight years inside a big, safe company, he unexpectedly found himself out on the streets. The career home he had constructed didn't exist any longer and the rest of the world had changed dramatically since he entered the bio dome of that job.

With a great sense of exasperation he said, "I don't even know how to use LinkedIn."

No one expects a sudden job change; that's why they are sudden. And if you've been employed for longer than a year, you've seen one happen—either to you or to someone you know. A corporate rogue wave caught some boat completely off guard.

In between the massive waves of drastic career change, there are other, less pressing problems that also threaten our work. Things like Career Ceilings.

A Career Ceiling is the lid on top of your career ladder. It's the top height any particular job path is going to take you. I ran into one when I was a senior content designer at a software company.

I started working there as a contractor. Over time, I earned a real position within the company and in a few years I was given a senior content designer title. That's when I had effectively come to the end of my career path.

I was making the most money I would ever make in that role and there were no other writing roles available at that company. Nor would there ever be. The only way up was to become a creative director, which meant managing designers and copywriters. That's a great option for some people but for me it meant doing a whole lot less of what I actually liked doing: writing.

I was thirty-two and my life had already gently rolled to a place of inertia. I might get small raises over the years to come and slightly more responsibility, but for the most part that was it.

My wife would later tell me she was deeply concerned. With two young kids, a mortgage and a fairly new marriage, it was intimidating to stare down thirty years of possible career monotony. I might not be that adventurous, but being "done" careerwise at thirty-two was a jagged little pill to swallow.

When you hit a Career Ceiling, you used to have only a few options. You could:

1. Get a job at another company.

2. Do a job you didn't want to do, like being a creative director.

3. Suck it up and die inside over a period of roughly thirty years.

The first option doesn't fix things, it just delays them. You might get a different title and more money. That other company might have a "senior senior writer" position but eventually you'll face the same ceiling you faced at your previous job.

In the second option you just trade your ladder for a different one. This plan doesn't work well because you end up doing more of something you didn't want to do in the first place. If you didn't want to be a creative director, progressing up that ladder wouldn't feel like a promotion, it would feel like punishment. You would just be going deeper into the wrong career.

The third option is definitely the most depressing but it's also the most popular. That's why in a 2013 Gallup survey, 70 percent of Americans said they hated their jobs or felt disengaged.[1] As a culture we've collectively bought into the lie that work has to be miserable. Dilbert books didn't sell millions of copies because people are happy at work. We eat at TGI Fridays not TGI Mondays.

We live for the weekends because we've accepted that the weekdays are where dreams go to die. Poke your head up if you're reading this book at work. Seven of the ten people you can see hate being there. No one wants to stay at a job they don't like.

What if it didn't have to be that way? What if having the job we wanted to have was about being the person we needed to be first? What if it wasn't about trying to avoid career transitions but instead embracing them? Because they are coming, for all of us. Every one of us will experience a Career Jump, a Career Bump, Career Ceiling or Career Opportunity.

How do we make wise Career Jumps?

How do we navigate the Career Bumps?

How do we break through the Career Ceilings?

How do we make the most of unexpected Career Opportunities?

Turns out the solution to all four questions is the same: We build a Career Savings Account.

■ Opening the Vault

Within twenty-four hours of leaving my last job one hundred different friends had reached out to me.

Within a week, I had a team helping me build a new blog.

Within a month I had new writing projects lined up.

This did not happen because I am amazing or have a thick, commanding head of hair. It happened because for five years I'd been making deposits into the tool kit I call my Career Savings Account.™ Since I'm bad at math, I came up with a very simple formula to explain the Career Savings Account (CSA).™

$$\left(\begin{array}{c} \text{Relationships} \\ + \\ \text{Skills} \\ + \\ \text{Character} \end{array} \right) \times \text{Hustle} = \text{Career Savings Account}$$

Put more Twittery:

(Gang + Awesome + Nice) × Grind =
Career Savings Account

What does each investment mean? Here's how we'll define them:

Relationships = Who you know. The gang you lock arms with during your career.

Skills = What you do. The tools you use to build your career.

Character = Who you are. The mortar that holds the entire CSA together.

Hustle = How you work. The fuel that pushes you to do the things other people don't, so you can enjoy the results other people won't.

You're already familiar with every part of the Career Savings Account. Regardless of your current job situation, you weren't surprised to hear that you need anything on that list. No one read it and thought, "Character? I've never thought to have that!"

You've also already applied aspects of the CSA to other parts of your life. You've worked on the skills of your golf game to get better. You hustled when you and your wife were dating to convince her you were the one. You've built relationships with sorority sisters who you still keep in touch with long after college ended.

The items aren't new, but the direction we focus them is. You already have most of the things you need for a Career Jump, Bump, Ceiling or Opportunity; you've just likely never applied them to your job.

Or, like me in the first seven years of my career, you haven't combined all four investments before. Maybe you're amazing at relationships and skills, but haven't mastered the art of hustle yet. Or you've got the type of character people write folk songs about but have never honed a set of skills. It's not that you have a bad career, but in the absence of one investment, the other three never reach their full potential.

Here's what happens if you only have three pieces of a Career Savings Account:

Relationships + Skills + Character – Hustle = Wasted Potential, NFL Draft Busts, One-Hit-Wonder Bands

Skills + Character + Hustle – Relationships = The Career Version of the Emperor's New Clothes

Character + Hustle + Relationships – Skills = Me in the NBA or Michael Jordan in Baseball

Relationships + Hustle + Skills – Character = Tiger Woods, Enron, Guns N' Roses

I didn't really even know I had been building a CSA until I saw how I was handling my jump and how people thought I should be handling it.

People would approach me with sad looks on their face, as if I had lost a limb. With quiet, concerned voices that sounded like chamomile tea they would ask me questions like,

"Are you guys going to move?"

"Is there anything we can do?"

"Could we just hold you awkwardly and cry together for a while?"

These were all nice questions, but they revealed an interesting belief: Someone who is in career transition should be devastated.

The reason most people think this is that they don't have anything to fall back on. An unexpected Career Do Over forces them to swing wide the doors of their vault and for the first time they are horrified at how empty it is. They've never created a Career Savings Account and didn't even know they needed one until they were desperate.

Why is that the case?

Because we were taught to work jobs, not build careers.

▦ Why We Ignore Our Careers

People often say it's not what you know, it's who you know. When I have a problem with my cable, I call the Comcast guy. When I have a problem with my computer system, I call my IT guy. When I have a problem with my money, I call my financial adviser.

In almost every single situation in life that you will face, there's someone you can call or e-mail for help.

Except for your career.

Except for the thing you do at least forty hours each week.

Except for that thing you're going to do in order to pay off a $100,000 student loan.

That area has few experts or counselors. It is by and large left vulnerable and unprotected. It is not because we are bad at seeking advice. And it's not that we're bad planners. Look at the way we approach saving for college.

If you haven't started a college fund for your child by the time you leave the maternity ward with that wrinkled raisin of a human, you are already behind. And probably a pretty lousy parent.

The second they emerge from the womb you have a great sense of dread that college is almost here. Every parent on the planet just makes you feel worse as they tell you constantly at dinner parties, "It goes by so fast. Kids grow up so fast! Dust in the wind."

You call your financial adviser and set up some sort of upside-down Roth IRA. (I'm sketchy on the specifics but I'm pretty sure my guy Jeff has used those words around me.) You start saving and paying off debt in preparation for college.

But that's not all. You also have to get your kids signed up for the right activities. When I was a kid, I spent my entire elementary school career just trying to jump my bike off of angled piles of dirt in the woods. Now though, each year the need to get a kid good activities for a college application starts earlier and earlier. My daughter spent one Saturday participating in the math Olympics. She's on a competitive math track, one that will prepare her for the future and hopefully college.

She was also in the fourth grade at the time.

We pull the college slingshot back so far until finally high school graduation comes and we release it. We head off to four or five amazing years. Our parents needed eighteen years to prepare for those and it is all worth it.

We graduate college, eventually find a job and then wait for the next career transition we'll prepare for, which turns out is retirement.

From the age of twenty-two to sixty-two this is the only thing we are taught to get ready for. We have conversations about our 401(k). We start paying for our house so we have somewhere to live when our jobs are over and our bones are brittle. We get disability insurance just in case we get hurt and can't work. We write living wills and get ready for the great beyond.

And we completely and utterly ignore the years between college and retirement.

We have a forty-year gap where we just get by.

We save for rainy days when it comes to our bank accounts but don't do anything to protect our careers from the storm.

Sure, there are some professions that have continuing education. I know real estate agents and financial advisers who work with life coaches and gurus. But for the vast majority of us, we have nowhere to turn if we feel stuck or have a career itch.

If you're a thirty-four-year-old Web developer right now and you feel like maybe you're in the wrong place careerwise, who are you going to call?

Although I'm a huge fan of personal counseling, I know for a lot of people that's not an option. There's a significant emotional span to cross if you think you'll just pick up the phone and ring up someone who tends to deal with personal crises.

Maybe you could call your friends. After all, they get it. They probably hate their jobs too. Maybe over coffee you can commiserate about the state of things. Misery loves company, but company often multiplies your misery. Quiet coffees in hipster spots usually change very little.

Perhaps you could just get on Twitter or Facebook and complain about your job as if public social media platforms are private. Ignore the fact that there are entire companies that exist to build background checks on employees, scraping everything you've done online. Right now, 80 percent of employers Google you before they bring you in for an interview.[2] Though whining online might provide temporary relief, you're also building a pretty good argument that you deserve to be underappreciated at the current job and not hired at the next one.

Maybe you go online and search "Career Help." The good news is, there are two billion results. The bad news is, there are two billion results. Where would you start? CareerBuilder, a site for posting your resume? An article on the Huffington Post about unconventional things you should be doing to get your dream career? A career coach? The first one I found charged $1.99 per minute, which seemed less like a career coach and more like a . . . racquetball instructor. You could always polish off a few skills you haven't thought about since the last time you looked at your resume and throw your hat in the ring. Only there are a lot of hats in there already.

So you hang up all the phones and go off-line and decide to suck it up for one more day. Or one more week or one more year.

You feel better, comforted by the fact that at least you tried. A deliberate Career Do Over is too complicated. It's just too fuzzy. It's just too hard to figure out.

It's not, though. The Career Savings Account makes a Do Over incredibly simple. All you have to do is combine things you already understand, like relationships and skills, and amplify them. You won't even have to face that many different types of career transitions either. There are actually only four.

■ The Four Types of Career Transition Everyone Faces

Have you ever felt overwhelmed at the very thought of having a Do Over? Maybe the idea of improving your career feels like entering a jungle full of thick vines, dangerous pitfalls and battling a resume you've done a pretty horrible job of updating. Fear not, our careers are not that complicated. In fact, there are only four career transitions you have to deal with and **this illustration** shows each one.

Sometimes, in your career, you will make **voluntary** decisions, like applying to a new job. At other times, forces outside your control, like an unexpected layoff, will impact your work in an **involuntary** way. Drawn north to south, this line captures every type of

The DoOver Chart

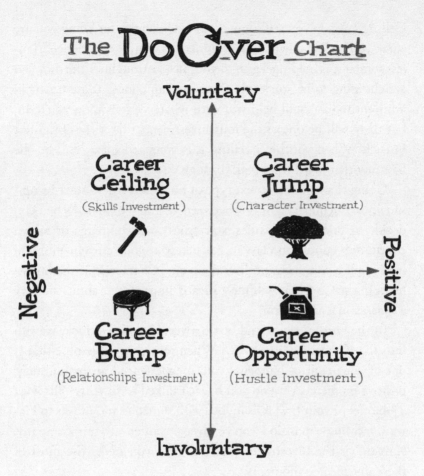

Voluntary

Career
Ceiling
(Skills Investment)

Career
Jump
(Character Investment)

Negative

Positive

Career
Bump
(Relationships Investment)

Career
Opportunity
(Hustle Investment)

Involuntary

career action you'll experience. But not every voluntary action is good; you might willingly stay at the wrong job out of fear. We all make bad decisions. We all have friends who voluntarily dated idiots much longer than they should have. Not every involuntary action is bad either. You might get an unexpected promotion at work.

In addition to the vertical line, representing voluntary to involuntary, there is a second line going horizontally from **negative** to **positive**. These two simple lines create four boxes, representing the four major career transitions you'll experience in life.

In the upper-left box, between 9 and 12 o'clock, is a "Career

Ceiling." When you willingly go to a job where you know you are stuck you are experiencing a "voluntary, negative experience." Unless someone is holding a gun to your head throughout the day, you are choosing to be stuck and therefore can choose to be unstuck! Your entire CSA will help you with whatever transition you're in, but there will be one of the four investments that shines brightest in each. When you hit a ceiling it is your skills that will be the hammer that helps you break through.

Going clockwise, the next type of transition is a "Career Jump," shown in the upper right box between 12 and 3 o'clock. When you decide to change companies, start your own company, or take a continuing education class to get better at your current job, you have made a voluntary, positive decision. "Character," is the investment in the CSA that will most greatly impact your ability to have a successful Career Jump.

In the bottom righthand box between 3 and 6 o'clock, we run into the "Career Opportunity." When something awesome that is out of your control happens, you've experienced an involuntary, positive moment. A friend you haven't talked to in years calls with a job offer or your boss falls in love with someone and moves to Hawaii vacating a position you've always wanted at your company. "Hustle" is the investment that will help you make the most of these unexpected moments.

In the bottom lefthand box between 6 and 9 o'clock is the "Career Bump." You got fired, lost your job in a layoff or graduated into an economy where approximately nineteen positions are available. It's an involuntary experience all right, but it's certainly not a positive one. "Relationships" are critical here because community is what will carry us through challenges like this.

Are the lines between these four transitions as neat as they were drawn in the illustration? Of course not; life is messier than that and the borders between something like a Career Jump and a

Career Opportunity can feel murky. With a well-funded CSA, though, you'll be ready for any of the career shifts you experience.

That's the best part of the Career Savings Account: You have the freedom to apply it to your unique situation. It isn't a tool for certain types of people with certain types of career aspirations. It's a tool to reinvent your work, no matter how you choose to personally define that goal.

▨ Two Things That Will Ruin Your Career Do Over

Fear does not fight alone.

I used to think it kicked down the doors or slid through the keyhole by itself. I spent years working with people around the country to help them face their fears. To the best of my abilities, I taught them some tricks about defeating the fear we all feel. We wrote them down. We responded to them with truth. We punched them in the face.

Unfortunately, fear has a friend. While I was feeling smug about defeating fear, something else was kicking people in the ribs. Something quieter and far subtler than the neon monster of fear.

The moment fear gave up the ghost, it tagged in its partner and something even more insidious stepped in the ring. Complacency.

And it starts so subtly, too.

Early on, we fight our fears. We get full of motivation. We read that book. Go to that event. Drink that brightly colored energy drink and jump into the air full of excitement. As our feet hit the ground though, we are promptly slapped in the mouth by the question "What next?"

We land on our feet after our celebratory fear-beating jump and don't really know where to begin. The fear might have subsided but very rarely is a plan left in its wake.

If we knew what to do next, exactly what to do, we would do it.

You'd be amazed at what we would do. Our fury and fire would rival the sun. But, what? What next? What now?

We don't have a perfect plan. Nobody does, but we think everybody does. And we don't want to make a mistake. You don't want to waste this moment on the wrong thing.

We pause for a minute, just to get our bearings, mind you. Just for the moment, to perhaps catch a breath. All the while we are completely unaware of how fast inertia sets in. Becoming stuck is never dramatic, because then we would wake up. Complacency is a slow gas leak, not a bomb blast. Like being robbed by a thief in the night who only steals a penny at a time, we awake to find the days have all gone somewhere.

Things aren't bad. We don't hate our jobs. They're OK.

They're fine, even.

Our job is fine.

Our boss is fine.

Our life is fine.

A fine life is fine.

We are fine with fine.

And so we grow comfortable.

This is not a bad thing. I like comfortable. But great lives are very rarely created in great comfort. You'll never hear a musician say, "Life finally got so comfortable and easy that I was able to create my best music."

The distance between comfortable and comatose is surprisingly short.

The bright light of our bravery dims.

Our hope congeals.

We become stuck.

We will have Career Bumps. Someone will take the option to be stuck out of our hands, for the moment, catapulting us into a brave new world when they fire us or lay us off. For a brief moment we will consider doing something different. Maybe that Career Bump was a gift in disguise. But finding a job like the job you just had is a lot easier than anything else right now. Bumps are no time to dream. We return to center.

New job. New business card. New title. Same fine. Eventually the same stuck.

Other times we will shake off the rust ourselves, spurred on by something louder than our complacency. We watch our parents retire into a world they were promised would exist at the end of their fine job, only it doesn't. Our kids drop a comment grenade about how we're never around because we travel so much for work. A co-worker makes an offhand comment about being a "lifer" and for a fleeting moment we see the thin shackle we have applied to ourselves. We become aware of our own career mortality, determined to do something more meaningful. We get focused and work. We clean our room and do mental push-ups.

We go for it, believing that with our leap into something new we have finally beaten our fear forever.

Day one of our new adventure behind us, we are shocked to learn the hardest lesson of chasing a dream. When you go for it, you don't escape fear, you land in it. Fear is not a dragon to be slain once, it's an ocean to be swum daily.

When you were stuck at that job, fear felt simply like a pond you had to cross. It was dark and perhaps mysterious, but you could see the other side. Having sworn you were made for something more, sworn you'd never let fear defeat you, you jumped believing your single act of boldness left the deep waters behind. Only to land in the Mariana Trench.

On the other side of a Career Jump is more fear than you've ever known before. And I swear, no one tells you this. Not your friends. Not your family. Not books. They sell you on the before, maybe the moment of beating that fear, but never the after.

The after doesn't sell books. Nobody wants the promise of deep water, they want sunsets and sailboats.

So you think you've made a mistake. If you'd made the right decision and chased the right dream, shouldn't you feel less fear, not more?

In those moments of doubt, fear launches an ad campaign for fine. Your fine life was easier. It wasn't this hard. It's always available. What would the harm be in going back on the shore? It wouldn't be giving up. You'd just be taking a break.

Complacency rolls its sluggish head and wakes back up, ready for its shift.

Most of us will spend most of our lives walking that same circle.

We are afraid of the unknown.

We grow stuck in the known.

If we fight fear and become brave, fear will concede the loss but mutter under its breath as we pass, "It's going to be really hard, maybe you should be complacent."

If we fight our inertia and hustle, complacency will concede the loss but mutter under its breath as we pass, "It's going to be really scary, maybe you should be afraid."

These two enemies hot potato us back and forth until we finally give up. We accept that Monday must be miserable. We buy the myth that there's a perfect job out there and quit a dozen great jobs in search of it the wrong way.

It wasn't always this way, though.

As kids we believed we had the power to declare "Do over!" when something didn't turn out the right way.

We'd stand in the street and boot a second attempt at kickball. We'd crumple up a piece of paper when the dog's head ended up lopsided and scribble all over on a new one.

We were not afraid to try again.

Somewhere along the way to adulthood we forgot we still have permission to do that.

And not just with art or neighborhood sports, but something much larger. Something that often owns our days and haunts our weekends. Our careers.

The good news is it's never too late to declare a Do Over.

All you need is a Career Savings Account.

With these four investments: relationships, skills, character and hustle, a Career Savings Account will help you rescue, reinvent and reenergize your work.

Sound like an overpromise? It's not, because now you know there are only four types of career change you have to face in life. Whether you're a thirteen-year-old with a paper route or a forty-three-year-old with a hedge fund we will all deal with the same handful of situations from our illustration.

You will hit a Career Ceiling and get stuck, requiring sharp skills to free yourself.

You will lose a job unexpectedly, requiring strong relationships to survive.

You will make a job jump, requiring solid character to push through the chaos stepping out always stirs up.

You will get a surprise opportunity you didn't see coming, requiring dedicated hustle to take advantage of it.

That's it, there are four types of major career change. And the Career Savings Account has an investment designed specifically to help you get the most out of each one.

Careers are built or broken on how we invest in them. That's why this book will help you do two things:

1. Build a Career Savings Account worth billions.

2. Spend it on the Career Do Over you've always wanted.

Careers are only difficult because they are constantly changing and we are not. We tend to hate change, despite the benefits it offers, and ignore it, deny it, or fight it and become stuck.

It's time to change the way we look at our careers.

It's time to chase the dreams we've been running from.

It's time to do work we care about.

It's time to get unstuck.

It's time to call a Do Over.

2

Do This First

I don't finish books. This is a shame, given my chosen profession of writing books, but there it is.

My shelves are piled high with books I've read thirty pages of. Even great books tend to die an early death in the face of the busyness of life. I'd love to think you'll finish this one, but there's a whole world of awesome things to do, like kite surfing, so let's not waste any time.

Fear and complacency will quickly erect two walls between you and your Career Savings Account should you declare a Do Over. The first wall is called attitude and the second is called expectations.

If you want to have a better job today, deal with both of those walls.

I can't teach you a new skill in the next thirty seconds that your boss will be blown away by. I can't change your character in the next paragraph. One page of words will not deeply impact your hustle on your dream or fix all your relationships, but if you want to have a better job right this second, that's possible. All you have to do is choose your attitude and adjust your expectations.

Notice I didn't say, "Change your attitude." That could take years. Choosing it, though, takes a handful of seconds. Tomorrow at work, choose to have a good attitude. Choose not to be cynical. Choose not to act like you're doing them a favor by showing up. Choose not to complain. Choose to cheer for the accomplishments of your coworkers. Choose to treat customers like superstars.

Choose your attitude every day until eventually it chooses you right back. It's not about feeling happy or feeling committed to your work or feeling like being a good employee. Feelings are the flightiest things in the world, held to the whimsy of a thousand factors. Feelings will tell you the day is already ruined because you woke up on the wrong side of the bed or had a bad commute that morning. Don't listen to feelings. Make choices. Today, choose a good attitude. This is the one thing you can do right this minute to actually shock your boss, improve your work relationships and dramatically increase your long-term odds of an awesome career.

The second thing you need to do is to adjust your expectations. What are you expecting your job to do for you? We all carry laundry lists of secret expectations, and when our jobs fail to meet them we fail to enjoy our work. Do you expect your job to fulfill every creative wish you have? Do you expect work to bend around your dreams and hopes? Do you expect that this will be the last job you have, since changing jobs is such a hassle? Take three minutes and write down what your expectations are for work. And then, take another three minutes and write down the real ones because you probably just lied to yourself a little bit.

Tom Magliozzi, the late cohost of NPR's *Car Talk* show, theorized that "Happiness Equals Reality Minus Expectations," but I disagree.[1] If you pull the thread of that thought, what it's saying is that "the way to be happy is to not have expectations," but that's ridiculous. To have an expectation is to have a hope. To have a dream. To have a desire about something you want to happen. Surely, deadening our ability to hope is not the solution to our frustration at work. The trick is not to eliminate your expectations; the trick is to adjust them.

Write them down and then find the right home for them. You may very well have some expectations that belong at your job. You may also have a lot of expectations that belong somewhere else. Like a side job or a hobby or a different job altogether. I've always wanted to write books of poetry. Was that the right expectation to place on my last boss, Dave Ramsey, a by-the-numbers financial guru? Probably not, but I still mistakenly did it.

When your attitude or expectations get out of whack you create a vicious cycle that cripples most Do Over moments. Your unspoken, unmet expectations give you a bad attitude. Your bad attitude makes you even more unreasonable in demanding that your job meets your expectations. You do enough laps around this circle and work becomes more miserable.

Want a better job right this second? Choose your attitude and adjust your expectations.

Investment 1
RELATIONSHIPS

Who you know.

Negative

Career
Bump

(Relationships Investment)

Involuntary

Investment 1: Relationships

I get by with a little help from my friends.

—THE BEATLES

I once worked for a company that paid employees $250 if someone they recommended got hired and stayed longer than ninety days. They paid $2,000 if the person referred was that mythical creature known as a "developer."

They did this because $2,000 was a small amount of money to pay for the right person. The wrong person is always more expensive, which is why Tony Hsieh, the CEO of Zappos, once estimated his bad hires have cost his company "well over $100 million."[1] Finding good people is difficult, and companies know that the fastest, cheapest way is often via a relationship.

Long before the term "hacking" was popular, the original way to hack a job search was to know someone. "It's not what you know, but who you know" might feel cliché but it's still true.

Relationships get you the first gig. They get you the first interview and opportunity. This is true because it's almost impossible to assess someone's character and hustle from a resume alone. Everyone who ever got fired in a job scandal had a decent resume that did not say, "Prone to embezzle money" or "Strong ability to come in late constantly, particularly on days we have important client meetings." Skills are a little easier to judge based on a resume but even those can be bedazzled.

Relationships provide the most accurate, immediate assessment of a job candidate. If you trust Bob, if you know he has character, skills and hustle and he recommends someone, you are more likely to believe that person has the same qualities Bob does. Bob has given him the Bob seal of approval, effectively putting his own reputation on the line for someone else. He's already personally vetted him or her.

Relationships not only help you get a new job, they help you get promoted at current jobs as friends tend to fight for friends much harder than just unknown names on a list of candidates. On the flip side, relationships will help you during involuntary, negative career transitions like getting laid off or fired. During Career Bumps, relationships will be the safety net that catches you.

We don't often spend intentional time building relationships because the return on investment doesn't feel immediate or measurable enough. We tend to focus on the things that feel more in our control, like skills and hustle. Neither of those carries the perceived messiness of relationships. But if your Career Savings Account is high on everything else and empty on relationships, you will become a career hermit. Hardworking, full of character, with skills galore, but not connected to anyone who loves you enough to tell you that you shouldn't wear a Hitler mustache in a Hanes commercial, Michael Jordan.

Is that what you want for your career? An underwear commercial where you rock the world's most awkward mustache? Me neither.

In this section, we'll learn the key ideas to strengthen current career relationships and build new ones.

3

You Don't Know Who You Know

It's better to hang out with people better than you. Pick out associates whose behavior is better than yours and you'll drift in that direction.
—WARREN BUFFETT

People hate change.

Not just emotionally, but physically as well. Our brains hate change. There are biological reactions to change that burst in our hearts and minds like fireworks we didn't even have to light. Upon being confronted with change, our first reaction is to brainstorm reasons it won't work.

I'm too old.

I don't have enough money.

It's too risky.

I'm not qualified enough.

Someone has already done that exact same thing.

There are worse jobs than the one I currently have.

I don't have any relationships that can help me with my career.

For minutes or maybe even lifetimes, we do our best to rally the troops around why we shouldn't do something. And this tends to be the approach we take for ourselves and even other people.

When we want a friend to do something that they are resistant to, what is the first thing we always ask them?

"Why don't you want to do that?"

This is a very common question, but it's unfortunately the wrong one to ask.

In his book *Instant Influence,* Michael V. Pantalon, PhD, says that when you ask someone a question like this, you unknowingly invite them to brainstorm new reasons they don't want to do something. That question is an invitation to sit in the no and work yourself up even more than you were before.[1]

Asking a boss "Why can't I work from home one day a week?" encourages her not to only list the reasons she already told you but to daydream up some new ones. We can't help but use our imaginations in a negative way when we start with a negative question.

The solution is to try just the opposite. Instead of launching a search party for opposition to an idea, you launch a search party for the opportunity. In the example of the flextime-resistant boss, you'd say, "What's one reason you could see me working from home as possibly a benefit to the company?" You don't need a thousand reasons, just a positive foothold on which to build.

Which brings us to the very first exercise in this book.

■ This Is Going to Feel Stupid and That's OK

There are a million ways to get stuck in a career, but every version shares one thing: a suspension of creativity. Our ability to dream and hope and desire a better job or a different job gets wounded. We turn off that part of ourselves that believes next Monday could be better than this Monday and instead accept our fate.

To start our Career Savings Account, we're going to begin with relationships and we're going to need the tiniest sliver of hope. The problem is that you don't know who you know when it comes to career relationships. You might be able to name five people you worked with at your last job, but if I asked you what casual friendships you made two jobs ago that might be able to help you, you'd go blank.

Recognizing we might need more than five random people in our corner, our next thought is about networking. And we despise networking. We imagine some mixer in a hotel conference room where anyone you make eye contact with throws their business card at your face. We instantly remember the most abusive networking person we've ever met and assume that dare we try to build better career relationships we will instantly become them.

We know networking is important, though, and in shame will ask ourselves, "Why do I hate networking?" or "Why don't I know anyone who can help me with my career?" At which point, much like Pantalon predicted, we'll start brainstorming reasons we hate networking with such a passion and are in fact the least connected person in our entire industry.

I'm with you, networking is miserable. Whenever I find myself at a dinner party where people are networking I immediately focus on the dog, and if the host doesn't have one, I focus on persuading them to get a dog.

So I assure you, there will be no cheesy networking ahead.

What I am about to share is focused on our careers. Does most of it apply to all types of relationships? I think it does, but this is not a relationship book. Though I would actually crush your online dating profile if you let me write it, I won't be giving broad relationship advice here.

And the tips in this section will not help you manipulate people into doing what you want. Approaches like that are part of the reason so many people are afraid to be deliberate with their relationships. Working on a relationship like a project feels disingenuous. But to believe that being intentional about a relationship is selfish or manipulative is to believe that being lazy about a relationship is humble and nobly motivated. Sure it is. If you're married, the next time your wife is hurt by you not doing something fun and planned out for your anniversary tell her you didn't want to manipulate the situation. Let me know how that goes.

Instead of networking or manipulating, we're just going to ask one impossibly simple question. We're going to suspend that part of ourselves that wants to immediately proclaim, "I don't know anyone who can help me. I have no friends. I have no contacts. I live in a hermetically sealed bubble and order my coffee online so as not to interact with humans."

Put that on pause for a minute and just answer this question:

Who is one person who could help me with my Career Do Over?

Write their name down in the margin of this page.

Don't you already feel like a tiny bit of a winner? That wasn't so hard. And the reality is, that was just the tip of the iceberg, because you already know a lot more people than you think.

▨ The Note Cards

If you visited the Acuff house during the writing of this book, you'd probably be surprised by the dining room. Although it's usually a fairly neat space, for three months it looked like the lair of a mad scientist. I didn't have beakers because that'd be weird and I'd probably have to order them online from a strange beaker company that would send me catalogs for the rest of my life. But I did have notes covering every wall.

It didn't start out that way. Initially, I did all my work on a laptop trying to outline everything in one massive Word document. It was fine at first, but the more I added to the outline, the harder it got to keep up. I couldn't quickly find what I had hidden in Chapter 3 or understand how Chapter 6 was going to resolve. It

was a frustrating exercise of scrolling and misplacing ideas. Finally, after probably our fiftieth confusing conversation, my wife, Jenny, had had enough. She grabbed something from the kitchen drawer, slammed it on the table like we were playing suburban dominos and said, "There!"

I stared at the table and laughed: note cards.

Of course, it always comes back to note cards. For years, we've used note cards to gain clarity in our biggest life decisions.

If you want to map something out, there is no greater tool.

Great thinkers the world over have known that forever. The only reason cavemen painted on walls was they didn't have note cards.

This isn't just crafty hyperbole either; there's gobs of research that shows how important it is to write out your ideas and see them. "Writing stimulates cells at the base of the brain, the reticular activating system (RAS). The RAS filters incoming information and attaches more importance to some information than to other information."[2] Since we're going to spend forty hours a week for forty years at a job, it behooves us to get our brains focusing in the best possible way on the ideas we'll be discussing going forward.

Throughout this book, I'm going to encourage you to grab some note cards for an exercise. If at any point you say, "I can't waste my money buying $5 note cards," I will ask if you have a $4 life? You will get mad and someone will probably get throat-chopped in the ensuing melee. Buying some note cards will be a lot easier and cheaper, too, though I'm not sure what the co-pay is on a throat chop.

If you've never done this exercise, I'm going to need a little leap of faith for this chapter. I know it's weird and I promise not to go all *A Beautiful Mind* with you, asking you to buy twine so we can connect the note cards next.

I also need you to ignore one specific voice of fear that will get loud right now. It's the one that will say, "You can't do an exercise like this because you don't even know what you want to do with your life." It will tell you in moments like this, "What's the point of working on your relationships if you don't have a dream or career plan yet?" And I will tell you that that question is a lie.

I will tell you that if you don't know exactly what you want to do with your life, you're just like me. I don't know exactly either. I like to make people laugh and think. How vague is that? But you know what, I've figured out how to spend more time doing that over the last five years using my Career Savings Account and you can too. Don't worry about that one insufferable friend who knew what they wanted to be since they were in the womb. That person is the exception, not the rule.

Work on your Career Savings Account despite not knowing what you want to be when you grow up. No, forget "despite," work on it *because* you don't know. If you strengthen relationships, learn new skills, build your character and amplify hustle do you think you'll be closer to understanding what you want to do with your life or further away?

Grab a stack of note cards, or at least a piece of 8½" × 11" paper you have torn into four rectangles.

If you don't have a Sharpie or a pen, go to a book signing. You can get them free there. I was once standing by myself at one, desperately waiting for anyone to buy my book. I was greatly encouraged when a gentleman approached my table, expecting to hear a story of how my writing changed his life forever. Instead, he said, "These pens free?" referring to the collection of pens I brought to sign books. I was dumbfounded and said, "Sure, I guess." He took a handful and left. I just gave you a way to get free pens—you're welcome.

Now that we've already dominated the "Do I know a single person?" exercise it's time to dive a little deeper. The reason we're doing this is that to strengthen our career relationships we have to know who we are in a relationship with. In later sections of the book we'll refer to these note cards. In the "Skills" section when we need an accountability partner to help us learn a new skill, selecting one will be a lot easier if we have a stack of note cards to pull from.

To begin, answer the following questions, starting with your closest relationships and then progressing to your most casual, writing one person's name per card. (I'm pretty sure you might be able to double, triple or even quintuple the results of the first exercise.)

1. Who do I know that is wise about career issues?

Who are the gurus in your life that your circle of friends tend to turn to for work advice? Who do you know that has excelled in their career that might be able to help you? I love that you have a friend who is really smart about marriage. I bet he has a beard. That's great, but I don't really care about him in the context of this conversation. Unless he's an influencer as defined in question three, I want you to focus on finding people who are wise about career issues, regardless of their specific industry.

2. Who have I worked with?

Right now, start writing down the names of people you've worked with in the last five to ten years. (Don't you dare get out the company directory and start transposing every name of every person employed by your company! Only the people you've worked with personally.) If you're in college and haven't had a full-time job yet, write down any part-time colleagues you've had and the names of professors who taught you. One name per card. Go.

3. Who do I know that is influential?

Every person has someone in their life who has influence. It doesn't have to be career driven because with this question I want you to start expanding the circle of names you're writing down. Take a wide view. For example, let's pretend you wanted to work in construction management. Your dream is to build homes. You scan the relationships section of your Career Savings Account and quickly realize you don't know anyone who builds homes. But what about plumbers? What about electricians? What about the people who serve the contractors who shop at the local Home Depot? You might not know someone directly in the construction management industry but you might know someone connected to it, someone who is influential. Maybe there's a friend of yours who is a connector; they simply know everyone. Are they involved directly in the construction industry? No, but you should still list them as an influencer. It's not just about getting to one circle of relationships, it's about getting to multiple. Maybe they have a second- or third-tier relationship that could be huge for you, and if you edit them out of this exercise, you will miss it.

4. Who do I know that owns a business?

I suppose these people could be listed in the influencers column but I called them out on purpose. Don't just list businesses that are related to your current career, as we're expanding our search for connections. List any and all business owners who you know. (Not "know," as in someone you're close friends with, but rather "know," as in someone you've had at least one interaction with.) For my list I would include Dan Banks, the owner of *9 Fruits,* a smoothie shop near me. Am I looking to get into a business where I mix whey protein in things? Not really, but business owners tend to know other business owners. And they know lots of customers. Chances are, there's only one or two degrees of separation between Dan and a business that better fits my skill set.

5. Who do I follow online that is in my desired career space?

I went to an event in 2011 where a very famous person with an amazing story chose instead to give a speech about the Internet. He extolled its many painfully obvious virtues saying things like "You can get the weather on it and stock reports." It was profoundly useless. I will therefore spare you that awkward moment by not telling you all the amazing people you can connect with on this thing called the World Wide Web. But know this, from celebrities in industries you care about who will tweet you back to Facebook career communities, there are a host of potential connections waiting for you online. Do you know business guru Jim Collins? No, but can you learn from him online and maybe even get a helpful tweet responded to even if you're not a social media expert? You can. To have the biggest, best CSA possible, it's important that you use social media to the best of your abilities. Social media played a big part in how I was able to make connections that eventually led to dozens of speaking gigs. Don't be afraid to write down a few note cards with the names of people you follow online. Remember, we started with close relationships and are now at the casual end of the spectrum.

6. What casual relationships am I forgetting that might have a career impact?

I don't care how many cards you have in front of you, there's someone you are forgetting. I'd encourage you to lean more toward the side of having too many right now. Do what Curt Anderson did. He was a songwriter who didn't know many people in Nashville when he moved, but after a few months, he was able to cowrite with someone who had won multiple Grammy awards. Think that interaction came from his agent or some industry connection? Nope. The guy he wrote with was a dad who brought his kids to swim at the pool where Curt was a lifeguard. That's about as casual as it gets.

How's that list coming?

Don't try to do it all alone or all at once. Feel free to scroll through Facebook, Twitter or even a good old-fashioned address book. Take a friend who knows you out to coffee and ask them those six questions about your life. (Write them down in a notebook instead of cards and transfer them later or people will think you're odd.)

More than likely your list is longer than you thought it would be. We all tend to know more people than we really think. If it's not, don't worry about it. You might have too rigidly answered the questions above. Go back again and loosen how tightly defined each of your answers is. Try to find an even more casual relationship than the lifeguard at your gym.

Did you double your initial list, which was one person? Chances are you did because the first principle of relationships is that you don't know who you know.

Now you do though, which means you can start doing something about it and putting those note cards to good use.

Remember

▪ Relationships get you the first gig.

▪ You don't know who you know unless you spend deliberate time focusing on your relationships.

▪ Dentists say, "Only floss the teeth you want to keep." The same is true of career relationships; only invest in the ones you want to keep.

4

Give Your Foes What
They Need Most

If hugging someone who is expecting a handshake was an Olympic sport, I would sweep gold. As a public speaker I often have to navigate this awkward limb exchange and no matter whether I lead with a handshake or hug, the other person is thinking the opposite.

I actually caught myself developing a nervous habit where I blurt out, "I think we're on hugging terms?," to people I haven't seen in a while before I hug them. I invented the phrase "hugging terms," which also might be an electronic pop duo from Copenhagen that specializes in soundscapes you're probably not ready for.

The hug-handshake exchange is uncomfortable, but that's nothing compared to what happens when we give the wrong thing to a relationship. Everyone's experienced that on a date. A close friend once confessed his undying affection for a girl he'd known for years and in response she told him, "Thank you so much for telling me that!" as if he had informed her of a way to save on her monthly cable bill.

The challenge is that you can't give a relationship what it needs unless you know what type of relationship it is. Fortunately, for our

40

purposes, work relationships aren't nearly as complicated as personal relationships. At this moment, Facebook has eleven different types of relationships you can be in. For work, there are basically only three you'll ever run into during your career.

■ Foe

A foe is someone who is actively working against your dream. Actively can mean they are publicly criticizing it, attacking it or discouraging you. They don't necessarily have to hate it, though. A foe could be someone who keeps you out drinking on nights you swore you would work. Would they call themselves a "foe"? No. They'd probably even call themselves your friend, but the results are the same. Their presence is an attack on what you are trying to accomplish with your Do Over.

■ Friend

A friend is someone who is aware of your Career Do Over, excited for you and willing to cheer you along the way. People who click "Like" on your Facebook updates about your job search are friends. The guy you get coffee with in the break room is a friend. The neighbor who asks how things are going with your new company is a friend. Everyone who texted me during my last Career Do Over is a friend. This is where 95 percent of your relationships are going to fall since this category can range from casual acquaintance to close friend.

■ Advocate

An advocate is someone who is significantly helping you shape the course of your career. They are a copilot in the Do Over. They are focused on doing dozens of things, many long term, to be part of your career. These people are rare, like white tigers but not as rare as, say, magicians who own white tigers. This can be a spouse, a mentor or a business partner. As far as the relationships go you will have the least amount of advocates but they will have the greatest direct impact on your Do Over.

Roughly everyone you encounter during your career will fit into one of those buckets. And you won't easily confuse the groups. Save for an unusual "Et, tu, Brute?" stabbed-in-the-back situation, in the average career you won't catch yourself saying, "Sheila is either my closest advocate or my most bitter foe. Let's see how Monday goes."

Right now, you should take all the relationships you identified in the last chapter and place them in one of these categories. This is easy to do if you wrote your career relationships on note cards. Simply draw a line across a piece of paper, write "Foe," "Friend" and "Advocate" at three different points and then start placing the cards under the right label. If you made a list instead of using note cards, go through each name and quickly write the correct type of relationship beside each name. If you did neither, why do you hate me and your career so much? Go back and do the exercise even if it feels like eating kale. I'm on your side. I hate kale, too. Kale chips taste exactly like regular chips if you've never tasted a regular chip. They're like eating burned pages of a novel. I know they're good for me though. So are the note card exercises. Do them!

We've now identified a bunch of our current relationships and categorized them. Let's rip the Band-Aid right off and start with the worst one first.

▪ Foes

I make it a habit to talk to cab drivers when I travel. If television has taught me anything, it's that 87 percent of them are filming reality shows. One afternoon a man named Raid Naji Hadab picked me up at Hobby Airport in Houston.

Originally from Iraq, he has lived in Texas with his wife and kids for the last five years. In the course of small talk, I asked him if he ever went back to his home country to see family. He said he couldn't because Al Qaeda was trying to kill him. That was not the answer I was expecting.

After working as a translator for Americans in Baghdad, Raid got branded as a traitor. He had to move his family six times around the city in a period of seven years to avoid death threats. When he finally got his visa approved to move to America he sent his wife and kids in a separate car to the airport. He waited at his house for fifteen minutes and then drove himself. Why? He was worried someone was going to assassinate him as he tried to escape the country. If he was going to die, he wanted to make sure his family wouldn't be killed in the cross fire.

Raid has real foes, which was kind of annoying because he ruined my ability to think I did. Right before he told me his story I was going to tell him mine about a stranger on Twitter who had been mean to me. One time I tweeted that the next time I came to Seattle I was going to bring my whole family, to which some guy responded, "The only thing you're bringing is creepiness." His assessment of my creepiness was confusing given that he was shirtless, shaved, oiled and tanned in his Twitter profile photo. I would have responded to him but my wife was with me. At her funeral I'm going to release a book called "Terrible things my wife wouldn't let me tweet." It will be sold in commemorative wheelbarrows because it will be so long given how many serious foes I have faced, much like Raid has.

Chances are, no one is trying to kill you at your current job. If they are, please read a book on Krav Maga, not this one.

You probably didn't even place a single person in the foes category. Part of the reason is that in the last chapter we were trying to find people who would help us with our Career Do Over. The very nature of that question should have prevented us from brainstorming too many foes.

But even if you don't have one in this category, you might someday have someone who makes a career transition difficult so let's figure out how to deal with them.

The best news, the news that should make you at least a little relieved, is that this category doesn't matter.

Unless the person placed in this category is your spouse or close family member, I'd prefer that we all just ignore this group of people. The best thing to give a foe is distance. Trying to turn foes into advocates or even friends is one of the stupidest ways to waste your time. Sometimes even family members have to be let go of. If I had a dollar for every time a friend tried to change the mind of a hateful dad, I could afford to send them to a therapist who would also tell them to let pleasing their dad go.

We should ignore most foes.

The problem of course is that we won't. Foes are sticky. The people who deserve the least amount of our time and energy tend to get the most. So telling you to simply "Get over it and move on" would be empty advice. Because you're not going to and neither am I. I put the shirtless Twitter guy in a book! It's hard to give our foes distance, even if deep down we all know that's what they need.

So how do we deal with our foes? I have a few ideas.

▪ Shrink Your Definition of the Word "Foe"

The first thing you need to do with your foe category is define it the right way. Again, a foe is someone actively working against the success of your Career Do Over. A stranger who tweets one mean thing or a friend who says one disparaging comment really isn't a foe (e.g., Shirtless Twitter guy). They might be a jerk, but it's hard to assume they are actively working against you just because they said one thing.

There's also a difference between a foe and an idiot. An idiot is consistently a jerk to everyone. A foe is someone focused solely on your untimely demise. If one of your coworkers is difficult to work with but they treat everyone the same way, they're not your foe. They're your annoyance. Welcome to the planet. Some people are annoying. We still have to work with them and if we label them a foe it makes it harder for us. If you see people as your adversaries, it's almost impossible to have a good working relationship with them.

Offices are certainly jam-packed with "climbers" as well, but are those people foes? Most of them are selfish and focused on their own rise, not necessarily your downfall. If your definition of foe is too loose and is essentially "anyone who kind of bothers me ever," your job is going to be miserable. You've painted everyone with this broad enemy brush, so of course you are going to hate that job. But be honest, is your job full of foes or are you simply wearing foe goggles?

Don't Search for Foes

We like foes for one simple reason: they confirm the fears we have inside.

Most of us, when faced with a Career Do Over, will have some doubts. We'll have worries, anxieties and fears about building a Career Savings Account. In the midst of that, we'll secretly start to hope we can find someone to confirm our worst fears. That's why misery loves company.

If I can find someone to agree with all the negative things I feel about myself and this Do Over, then I don't have to do it. It's almost a relief when you can identify a hater. It's like the fear inside of you says, "See! That's a second person that feels you can't do it. Now we have a consensus! You have to quit!"

If you live like that long enough, you develop an itchy trigger finger when it comes to foes. Don't. Put the gun down. Stop searching for foes.

Compare the Internet to Real Life

Chances are, if you have someone who criticizes you, it's going to happen online. Someone you don't know well will say something negative about your life. They comment and hurt your feelings in some way. And you take it. You accept it, think about it and maybe obsess about it.

The next time you think about doing whatever it was that they had commented on (writing a blog, sharing a photo, dreaming out loud), you'll hesitate, recalling his or her words. Such is the power of the Internet. But if that person had marched into your cubicle at work and said what they said online in real life, you would have laughed them out of the room. Who are they to tell you how to live your life? They don't even know you.

That's the problem, we don't ever treat social media the way we treat the rest of our lives. When a stranger criticizes your entire life because of one thing you posted on Facebook, that's like someone driving by your house and yelling from his car, "Your yard is horrible, I bet your heart is too!"

You wouldn't listen to that person. You'd think, "Wow, that guy was crazy. Who yells mean things at strangers?" But online we act like Mark324DragonHeart knows us. He doesn't. Apply the "Real-Life Filter" and most online critics will disappear.

What Most Foes Are Yelling

So we've established two things: 1. You probably have a lot fewer foes than you think. 2. If your online foes happened to you in real life, you'd ignore them.

But what of the real ones? What do we do with the friends, co-workers or family members who are working against the success of your Do Over? The first thing is to understand whether these foes are clueless or calculated.

A clueless foe is that person whose behavior encourages you to fail. They are not malicious. They are not trying to make you lose, but with the power of their influence you are. Friends like this can accidentally do terrific damage to your ability to have a Do Over. In the book *Change Anything*, a team of authors discussed this very thing. They said, "Bad habits are almost always a social disease—if those around us model and encourage them, we'll almost always fall prey. Turn 'accomplices' into 'friends' and you can be two-thirds more likely to succeed."[1]

One of the easiest and fastest ways to turn an accomplice into a friend is to simply tell your accomplice what you are working on. Most of the time just the act of telling someone what you are trying to do with your life changes things. The key is not to attack the person but to just honestly say what you're trying to do and how you'd love his or her help. More than likely, he or she will say, "I had no idea I was tripping you up like that, I'd love to help."

Now some might not react that way. Some people like the old you. They don't want you to change and they certainly don't want to change themselves to help you with the process. Why does this happen? Sometimes, they're just mad that you are changing and they are not.

My daughter reminded me of that once at the grocery store.

As we left the store and entered the parking lot, I decided to ride the cart.

Why?

Because awesome.

As I was riding on it, my feet on the bottom, my hands holding the handle, I heard my ten-year-old yell something from behind me.

"Daddy, stop doing that! You're making us jealous!"

I thought that was interesting. She didn't yell, "Daddy, be careful!" She didn't yell, "Daddy, that's against the rules!" She yelled, "You're making us jealous!"

And there lies a simple truth.

Sometimes, people who hate on your dream aren't really mad about your dream. They're mad because you're making them jealous. They want to be the one feeling the wind in their hair as they ride through a parking lot. They want to be the one giving that speech or opening that business.

But for whatever reason, they aren't, and they have too much self-awareness to yell the truth like a ten-year-old. So instead they tell you it will never work or you need to be more realistic or you're being selfish. We have a thousand ways to play dress up with our jealousy.

So maybe a foe isn't any more complicated than a little kid in a parking lot who thinks that walking is way more boring than riding on a cart. If that's the case, next time you get hated on, remember what a lot of your foes are really saying.

"Stop chasing your dream. You're making us jealous!"

And in response give them the only gift we can give our foes—distance.

■ Stop Hanging Out with Lobsters

While writing this book, I went to Rockport, Massachusetts. Think for a second about the most scenic New England coastal community you can imagine, multiply that by one bowl of clam chowder, and you've got a picture of Rockport.

Nestled against the North Atlantic, the favorite feature of tourists is the long strip of shops and art galleries that stretches out into the water. This scenic street forms a "U" in the ocean providing a safe harbor for sailboats and lobstermen.

While walking around I saw a pile of old, colorful lobster traps. There were stacks of them stuck behind a store next to the harbor. I've seen old lobster traps before but there was something different about these. The difference was the birds.

Inside each old cage, birds were building nests.

Dozens of sparrows were flying in and out of the traps with pieces of straw. It was interesting to watch, like some sort of fowl construction site. Birds, the original hipsters, using found materials, locally sourced, to build a residence in an unexpected location. They weren't building nests, they were gentrifying lobster cages.

I started to think that if you asked a lobster if that was a good place to build a nest, they'd probably tell you no. That trap was death. For a lobster, going inside that trap was the last decision they'd ever make. Their entire lives were spent trying to avoid lobster cages.

And yet, for the bird, that cage was perfect. It was open and airy, but completely protected from cats. Cats, that I am aware of, do not know how to operate lobster cages. They were sturdy, stable and easy-to-get-into-and-out-of homes.

What was a cage to a lobster was a home to a bird.

Regardless though, the lobsters do not understand.

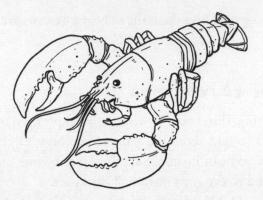

And right now, you've got some lobsters in your life, too.

Every job has lobsters, that group of people who are determined to hate the entire experience of working somewhere. I used to be a lobster, quick to criticize everything, slow to see anything good, determined to make sure everyone around me was having the same negative experience at work I was. I remember, with shame, when a friend and I took a new employee out to lunch at a job once. He was full of that new job buzz and we did everything we could to tell him how horrible the job he had just taken really was. We tried to clip his wings.

Misery loves company and it also recruits it. You have a gossiping, cynical group of lobsters that all go to lunch together at the company you're at right now. They're fun to hang around with sometimes—negativity is more enjoyable than we like to admit—but it's death to a Career Do Over. Hanging out with lobsters never teaches you how to be a better bird. That empties your Career Savings Account instead of filling it up.

Give the lobsters in your life what they really need. Distance.

■ What About Bad Bosses?

Bad bosses exist. I've had one or two in my day. When you realize that your boss is a foe, there are a few things you can do.

1. Improve your work performance to see if it improves your relationship.

You can't change someone, but you can impact a work relationship sometimes if you improve your work performance. Making a horrible boss's life easier by doing better work can often turn a horrible boss into a less horrible boss. Choose your attitude, adjust your expectations and apply the techniques in the hustle section of this book to see if you can level things out.

2. Admit you're an employee.

Sometimes when people tell me they have a bad boss, what they're really saying is "Who do they think they are to tell me to do that project?" At which point I say, "They are your boss, they are 100 percent of the people paying you money to tell you to do things. That's kind of how jobs work." I have a lot of short, awkward conversations that don't end in hugs or handshakes. If you have a boss who changes the time you get to go to lunch, guess what? She gets to do that. Is it fair? Is it fun? Is it right? Maybe not, but it's definitely a consequence of being an employee. If that's frustrating to you, move on to number 3.

3. Turn the frustration into fuel.

Do you know what every bad boss is really saying? "I dare you to get a better job!" Take them up on the dare. Forget gossiping and complaining, those don't get you anywhere. If your boss moves your lunch break to a time different from all your coworkers as some sort of passive-aggressive punishment, rewrite what she's really saying. She said, "Ha! You don't get to go to lunch with your friends for three weeks," but I swear you heard, "I dare you to use those quiet lunch breaks without your friends to apply to jobs!" Answer that dare.

Remember

- Be honest about your definition of the word "foe." If it's too large, admit it, shrink it and stop labeling so many people as foes.

- Don't look for foes who will confirm your fears that you're not qualified for a Do Over. You are qualified.

- Most foes are really yelling, "Stop chasing your dreams! You're making me jealous."

- Give foes what they need the most—distance.

5

Casual Counts

I hope you have a friend you can cry with. Someone who just gets you, you know? A gal pal, a sister who has traveling pants, a wingman, a buckaroo, a "Here's my kidney, man, you take it" kind of person. That is awesome for the forty hours you're not at work. But when you're in the career zone, I'm not worried about someone jumping on a grenade for you. I'm worried about someone sharing your resume for you.

I used to think in order to have a rock solid career, you needed to have rock solid friendships. That just seems like what you're supposed to tell people, wind beneath my wings and whatnot. Then I started to actually look at my own career.

Brannon Golden, who I'd met one time, edited my first book. Casual friendship.

Beth Corbett, who I worked with for six months, copyedited my first book. Casual friendship.

Shauna Callaghan, who I met once, built my blog after my last Career Do Over. Casual friendship.

Andy Traub, who I'd known mainly via the Internet, helped me get back up on my feet after my last Do Over. Casual friendship.

Shawn Hanks, who I hadn't seen in a year, helped me kick-start my speaking career after my last Do Over. Casual friendship.

My tender heart tried to remember that moment of lifelong friends rallying around me during my career transition, but the truth is that many of the relationships that did the heaviest lifting were casual at first. Which doesn't mean superficial.

Take Billy Ivey.

I saw him once in a nine-year period. We worked together at a company for about twelve months in 1999. In 2010, I helped get him an amazing job. Why? Because absence makes the heart grow fonder. No, because I knew he was a good writer and I knew a company that needed a good writer.

Casual counts, especially for our Career Savings Account. Those relationships have the tendency to level the playing field. You'll need heart friends, for certain. Those are great. Kidneys! But if you go through a Career Bump, which is when you need relationships the most, I want you to have a massive collection of casual relationships to fall back on.

■ Throw as Many Boomerangs as Possible

Do you know which career relationship is not going to matter to your job someday? No, you don't. Somebody you haven't thought about in years is going to help you. You're going to get a job from a cousin, or a friend of the sister of Ferris Bueller. If it hasn't

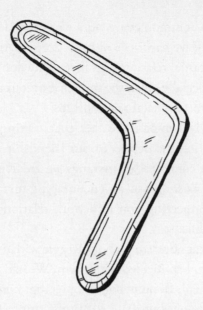

happened yet, it's going to. And if you want it to happen faster, you need to throw as many boomerangs as possible.

Boomerangs are work relationships that don't end, they just head off into the distance for a while. You're not mad at the person, there's no work relationship breakup ceremony. Some coworker you knew went off into the horizon and you went in the other direction. And someday, when you least expect it, they're going to boomerang back into your life with a work opportunity.

That's what happened with my biggest client, Reggie Joiner. In 2004 I applied to work at his company. I threw a boomerang. Nothing. A few years later, I sent some of my writing samples to his company through a mutual friend. Nothing. A few years after that I met him backstage after an event. Years after that I spoke at one of his events. Then we had lunch. And coffee. Then on the day I went through my last Do Over, he called and helped me navigate it. We'd seen each other three times that year.

Didn't matter, close relationships always start off casually. That's the one thing in common every close working relationship has. So why do we think we can rush right to deep relationships without having a ton of casual relationships first? Why don't we throw more boomerangs, especially given the immense amount of tools we have these days that foster casual relationships?

We constantly bemoan the fact that texting, Facebook and Twitter are eroding the depths of our friendships. That might be true but when it comes to boomerangs we are living in the golden age! Something as simple as an encouraging text or tweet can do wonders in reconnecting you to a work relationship you haven't talked to in a while.

I could tell that same story about Reggie with a handful of other people in my life. I connected with them. We had lunch. I spoke at an event with them. Boomerang, boomerang, boomerang. They're not a client right now, but that's the funny thing about boomerang relationships, you don't control when they come back.

But if you don't throw any, you are guaranteeing you won't have any that do.

■ Casual Relationships Run on Information and Queso

Unless your friend is lactose intolerant, I don't know if there's a better way to really form a perfectly casual relationship than over a bowl of queso.

But in addition to bowls of melted heaven, the thing casual relationships need the most is information.

If people don't know you need help, they can't help you.

Hate asking people for help? Me too. I'd rather not need it in the first place. Trust me, if I could curl up into a tight little ball like an armadillo and roll through my career perfectly without ever needing help from anyone else, I would. But I can't; neither can you.

We don't ask for help because we think we're the only ones who need it. We compare the manicured Instagram feeds of our friends to the messy reality of our own lives and come up lacking. We think everyone else has it all figured out so we pretend to as well.

If we ever investigated the lives of anyone successful we'd realize they never accomplished what they have all alone. Star quarterbacks have linemen. Steve Jobs didn't design the iPhone by himself. Oprah doesn't run the cameras.

We all need people to help us and the only way they can, especially casual relationships, is if we give them information. Not all of the information. The best way to end a casual relationship is to turn a fire hose on it. But just tell them the truth. If you're looking for a new job, tell them that. If you need a connection to someone else, tell them that. Our friends aren't mind readers.

Carlos Whittaker spent years building casual relationships across the country as a musician. He sang and played at hundreds of events. Eventually he decided that public speaking, not singing, was a Do Over he wanted to launch. The only problem was that everyone knew him as Carlos the singer, not Carlos the speaker. No one was booking him to talk. I asked him, "Did you tell your network of friends that you're focusing on speaking right now?" He said, "No." I then said, "Well then how are they supposed to know you are?" He sent out a simple e-mail explaining his Do Over and started to fill his calendar with the right type of opportunities.

Whether you're chasing a new dream or trying to climb the ladder at work, casual relationships won't know how to help us unless we ask for help.

Have you asked yet?

■ Start with a Small Table

I'm an introvert, which means I'll throw you out of my house if you try to linger much longer after we've served the "almost time for you to leave," postdinner coffee.

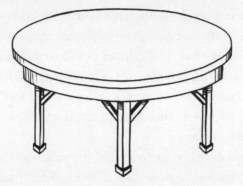

I don't grab anyone by the scruff of the neck, I just stand up abruptly midconversation and declare, "It was wonderful seeing you tonight!" The trick is to say it with enough confidence that it's clear you are reminiscing about an experience that has ended.

The idea of making new casual friends makes me feel anxious. I'm the one writing the book and even I feel like there might be some sort of corporate speed dating about to be sprung on us both in the following pages. "Greg is a computer programmer from Fresno who might one day become one of your advocates. He likes long walks on the beach and wolves."

Though I wish I was as passionate about anything in my life as people who are into wolves are about wolves, that's not where we're headed. If you want to have more boomerang relationships in your life, you don't have to come up with a complicated plan. You just have to find a table.

That's what Sarah Harmeyer did in Dallas, Texas, when she was new to the area and didn't know many people. She put a table that would seat twenty people in her backyard.

Realizing she wanted to know her neighbors, she simply invited them to dinner. All of them. She knew two at the time but figured that the worst that would happen is that no one would come to dinner that night. So, one by one she put invitations in their mailboxes, inviting them to a potluck. She expected a handful of people to show up. Instead, ninety-one people walked down her driveway that night.

She discovered what you'll discover if you dare to be just a tiny bit brave. People are desperate for community. All of us, even us introverts. Mark it up to fear, the pace of life or any other factor that whittles away at our sense of community; it feels hard to find these days.

So when someone risks awkwardness and dares to throw one boomerang, something strange happens: Other boomerangs show up. Or in Sarah's case, 1,500. That's how many people have come to dinner in her backyard since 2012.

The invitation process is simple. If Sarah meets a stranger at a cocktail party or the grocery store and they ask her what she does, she says, "What I love to do is something called 'Neighbor's Table.'" That's it, there's no VIP list, just new friendships starting around a big table. If you want to join her, visit NeighborStable .com. You could also swing by your local West Elm furniture store. Sarah's simple idea is so infectious they've asked her to throw Neighbor's Table events in some of their stores.

"I have so many friends in Dallas now," she says. "Some of my best friends I've met at the table."

You don't need to start with a table that fits twenty people. Sarah likes gathering people, that's one of her strengths, but we all need a table of some sort. Maybe your table is a pedestal at a meet and greet for people in your industry. Maybe your table is in the break room at lunch and it's a bagel with a coworker you don't know well. Maybe your table is a class in a subject related to your career at the entrepreneur center in your city. Tables come in a million shapes, but they all share one thing: community happens around them. Boomerangs begin across them.

If you have a hard time with the concept of starting a new relationship, find a table first.

■ Make New Casual Relationships. On Purpose.

We need to clear up a quick misconception. Casual doesn't mean accidental. Casual can actually mean on purpose if you deliberately choose someone you want to be friends with.

Did you know that we were able to do that? To just up and decide to be friends with someone and then go be friends with them? I've always thought career friendships grew organically, in a field somewhere and a stork brought them to your cubicle at work. One day you look up and there's a guy who's amazing at coding apps in a wolf sweatshirt standing there. Friendship!

That might happen—not the stork part—but the accidental friend at work who becomes a good friend over time. But it's a lot faster to choose who you want to be friends with.

Does that feel messy and undefined? Good. Relationships, especially new ones, are. I don't know what criteria you like to use when it comes to friends. Maybe you're an introvert looking for other introverts not to congregate with. The only criteria I use is "Who would it be fun to get to know?" I use that criteria because it helps me steer clear of the ladder-climbing first thought of "Who can help me the most in this room?" Has that ever happened to you at a dinner party? The person you're talking with is constantly scanning over your shoulder in hopes of upgrading the conversation by jumping to someone else? Ugh.

So I just try to find people who would be fun to get to know. Will they impact my career someday? Will they become an advocate? Will we work on a project together? Maybe, maybe not. Thankfully, it's impossible to predict that at the start of a friendship. (I can predict that 100 percent of the relationships I don't intentionally participate in go nowhere though.) Some of your most helpful work relationships didn't start out as a master plan to form a union that would change the world. You just thought it was fun to hang out with Mark, so you did. At the very worst, if nothing comes of my new friendships, I got to have a lot more fun than my week would otherwise have had. That's a win.

▪ Be a First Responder

Do you have a friend who won't ever answer the phone when you call? She doesn't completely ignore you. She does call you back, but only when it's convenient to her.

If you want to move beyond casual friendships at work, be a first responder. Don't sit on e-mails for days. Don't let voicemails log-jam on your phone. Don't force people to use multiple forms of communication to finally penetrate the ivory tower, or gray-walled cubicle you've hidden away in.

People hate having to ask this question: "Did you get the e-mail I sent you?" Which then forces you to admit, "Yes, I ignored it" or to say the lie we're all using right now: "No, my spam folder must have blocked it." We throw that spam folder under the bus constantly.

Pick up on the first ring. Answer the first e-mail. Those aren't just forms of communication, those are boomerangs from other people. Want more of the ones you throw to come back? Return more of the ones other people threw. Be a first responder.

▪ Own the Inconvenience

Want your friendships with the people you help, and who can help you, to get a little stronger? Increase the frequency of your interactions. You can't say, "It's weird, I only see Tom four times a year and it feels like we're not very good friends." One of the best ways to increase the frequency is to own the inconvenience of being friends.

Friendships built on selfishness never work out. If you want to have better friends, increase the frequency you see them on their terms, not yours.

I once caught myself only accepting coffee meetings at one of two places: Good Cup and Frothy Monkey. I did this not because I loved either place, though I do, but because those two places are the closest to my house. (And I knew how to park there. Showing up somewhere new and not understanding the parking is one of my deepest, weirdest fears.) I suggested those two locations out of convenience to me, not my friends.

When a coworker you want to be friends with suggests going out to Indian at lunch, don't refuse. Go to Indian. When someone asks you to help them run an errand that is out of the way, go out of the way. Pick up someone at the airport, carry couches up stairs and pivot! Own the inconvenience.

Remember

- Casual counts. Throw as many boomerangs as possible.

- Casual relationships run on (and deepen) based on your willingness to share information.

- If you need help with your career, ask for it.

- Everyone is looking for community. Start one by finding a table first.

- Want to be a better friend with someone? Be a first responder and own the inconvenience of the relationship.

6

Great Careers Take Great Advocates

It's one of my theories that when people give you advice,
they're really just talking to themselves in the past.
—STEVE GARGUILO

A friend is someone you share your day with.

An advocate is someone you shape your career with.

Although every advocate is a friend, not every friend will be an advocate. You know lots of people who you enjoy as friends but would not request career advice from. They are hilarious, fun to be with, maybe even close friends, but if you had a list of four to six people who helped steer the future of your career, you wouldn't put them on that list.

Like me and lumberjacking, which I'm pretty sure is how you verb that profession. My dad and I had a lot of fun the day we bought a chainsaw to cut down trees in our yard but you wouldn't want to ask us to be your lumberjack advocate. Our neighbor's roof and the tree we sent through it would tell you that, too. My role was to use a dental floss-thick thread to attempt to pull eight hundred pounds of angry timber away from the house next door as it sped toward the earth. I failed.

And so would you if you picked me to help you with your logging dreams.

A good advocate can be a business partner, former college roommate, old manager at a company you no longer work at, spouse or a million other people. But they all must have these three character traits:

1. They have to be brave.

It's fun when scores of friends clap and cheer for you. But there are times in life when you need more than just a cheerleader. You need someone who is brave enough to tell you the truth. Like an advocate. One of the greatest ways to ruin your Do Over is to surround yourself with people who can't tell you no. If you want to survive your next Do Over, make sure your advocates have the freedom to tell you when an idea isn't any good.

2. They have to be respected.

An advocate you don't respect isn't an advocate. We tend to discount the advice of people we don't respect, even if it's good advice. When they tell us something we don't want to hear, we can easily ignore it. "What do they know anyway? They're not up on my level." It's always best to find an advocate who you respect, or even better, who is better than you. Great people surround themselves with greater people who challenge and stretch them. A great advocate is a tuxedo, not a pair of sweatpants.

3. They have to be trustworthy.

At the base level, you must be able to trust that the advocate wants the best for your life. You have to be able to believe that regardless

of his/her advice and input, it all comes back to that. They want to see you do the most with your Career Savings Account and live up to your potential. That has to be the motive they are leading with or the whole thing falls apart. That's why it's almost impossible for someone whose livelihood depends on you to be your advocate. I can't tell you an unbiased truth about your career if my career depends on you. At some level my input will be tempered by "If I tell her this, will I get fired? Will it decrease the profits that impact my bonus? Will it jeopardize my job?" You might have an advocate you work on projects with as peers, but if you're the boss, don't expect your employees to sit on your personal board of advisers. They already sit on one of your boards; it's called payroll.

In addition to character, it's also critical that your advocates have significant skills, or in this case, the cheat codes.

▪ Cheat Codes Make the Game a Lot Easier

Outkast is one of the greatest hip-hop groups of the last fifteen years. They're the reason a generation that grew up without Polaroids knows how to "shake it like a Polaroid picture"; they've sold millions of albums and helped establish Atlanta as a new center of rap.

Along the way, crazily colorful, seemingly from another planet André 3000 (a.k.a. André Benjamin) has become a force to be reckoned with. He's moved from rapper to actor to designer, finding pockets of success at every turn. He also understands the value of advocates, or in his words, "mentors," like few other artists. That wasn't always the case, though. He says, "I didn't even know that word [mentor] until five or six years ago."[1] But now that he's experienced that type of relationship in his thirties, he knows one of the best reasons to work with someone further along than you is that they know all the cheat codes.

Here's how he describes the word "mentor" to his son.

"Adults are really cool and I'll tell you why. Because you can compare them to a video game. If you played that video game for the last two years and you're proficient at it and I just jump on the game, you're going to quickly say: 'Hey, Dad, the trap is right there. When you get over there, you have to go, hop, hop, hop, hop.' Now, if you didn't say that, it might take me a year to figure that out. So a mentor is: 'I've done this, so I'm helping you get past that place.'"[2]

He's right. Advocates and mentors know all the cheat codes. Here's the crazy part: If you'll listen, they will give them to you.

One afternoon, after giving a speech that fell flat to a room full of teenagers, a comedy group called the Skit Guys asked me if I wanted to know what the problem was. I said yes, because I wanted to get better at public speaking. They told me the house lights were too bright. Teenagers are nervous about laughing at the wrong thing. They don't want to feel embarrassed or look dumb. So if the room is bright, they won't laugh. (Adults are similar, which is part of the reason comedy clubs are so dark.)

Three hours later I gave another speech to the same group of teenagers. The content was similar, my delivery was similar, and my jokes were similar. The only thing different was that the room was darker. And the room exploded with laughter.

I didn't get dramatically better in the three hours between speeches. I got the cheat codes from an advocate. That's why you and I need them so desperately.

Want to grow the skills portion of your Career Savings Account quickly? Ask advocates for the cheat codes!

■ What Do Advocates Need?

We know what we need in an advocate (bravery, respect and trust), we know why we need them (cheat codes), but what do they need from us?

Foes need distance.

Friends need information.

Advocates need access.

An advocate is only as good as the amount of access you are willing to give them into your life. The best advocate for your career can't do anything if you stay surface level with them. That's why you have to trust them. They don't need to give advice to the best you, but rather the real you. It'd be like straightening your house before a cleaning person came over to tidy up. You're not trying to impress your advocates, you're trying to learn from them.

Access is easy to write about, but hard to actually give. It takes time. The three character traits advocates require—bravery, respect, and trust—all take time to recognize. Go slow, you can't microwave advocate relationships. Avoid the temptation to over-share, ripping your button-down shirt open in a Michael Jackson-like rage in the middle of the break room proclaiming, "This is my whole career! Who wants access to it?"

Take a look at the note cards you made for your relationships. Who did you put in the advocate category? If you have a few cards selected, decide one thing you might be able to share with them in regard to your career. Hint: It's not your salary. Sharing specific numbers about the money you make is black belt–level advocacy. Start slow. Give them access over time.

▪ Expand Your Definition of the Word "Expert"

Sometimes it's hard to find an advocate because we have a razor-thin definition of the word "expert." We hear that we need some-one wise to provide guidance and immediately think of Splinter, the talking sensei rat from Teenage Mutant Ninja Turtles. Not your first point of reference when you think of an expert? We're different.

To surface some advocates in your life, expand your definition of expert with these three categories:

1. Industry expertise

2. Life expertise

3. You expertise

The first one is rather simple. If you want to get great advice about being a better dentist, you should find an advocate who is ten years further down the road of dentistry. I'm glad your mom is a good listener, but if she's never been a dentist, it would be foolish to expect her to give you specific feedback on the latest laser treatments used in cleaning.

The second expertise advocates can possess is life experience. Trying to grow your dental business? A business owner in a different industry who is fifteen years older than you, with the kind of career success you hope to one day have, can teach you a lot. It doesn't matter that they've never peered into someone's mouth with sharp tools, they've spent years understanding the ins and outs of things like finding new customers. They've got a lot to show you. Don't define expertise too narrowly either. Dave Barnes is a musician, which seems different from being an author, but he's spent twelve years growing his career on his own. I could learn a ton from him about how to sell products (albums or books) at events.

The third area of expertise, you, might seem a little silly, but it's as worthy as the other two. Close friends who know you well can provide critical feedback as advocates. Even if they're your age, they've spent years becoming experts in you. They'll know that your desire to add another dental office to your practice is a product of ego, not of business savvy, and can point that out. This is why a spouse or a best friend can be an advocate.

The line between friend and advocate can be blurry sometimes. The other main difference between a friend and an advocate is that advocacy tends to be a one-way street, while friendship is reciprocal. The job of an advocate is to give you advice. Your job is to act on it. It's deliberately one-sided. A friendship, on the other hand, goes back and forth. If you treated a friend like an advocate, constantly asking for career feedback and wisdom, never repaying it, you'd be selfish. Friendships are about mutually sharing life.

With an advocate though, the expectations are just the opposite. I have a handful of people whom I get advice from. We've never met all together, but when I get to hang out with them individually I'm there to learn from them. It's not selfish for you to use the entire hour asking questions about your career situation. That's the whole point of having a career advocate.

Author Annie Downs meets with her board of advisers once a quarter. She selected and invited each member of her board over a period of months. She prepares an agenda and walks them through specific career challenges and opportunities she is facing. (Notice, no one in the room would be surprised that Annie wants to talk about Annie; they are advocates. She set clear expectations about the purpose of the team and members would be surprised if Annie suddenly said, "Enough about me, tell me about any challenges you're having raising your kids.")

I do not believe her board has a crest of some sort but they should. Annie is awesome.

I am not ready to be Annie and you might not be either.

The first thing we're going to build is an "invisible board" of advocates. They are invisible because at first the only one who will know they are an advocate is you. Without any sort of complicated selection process or weird mentor rose ceremony, we're just going to grab coffee with one of the people you came up with when you reviewed your note cards. From the shadows of "Is Jon Acuff going to make me do awkward things this entire book?" we're going to quietly build a secret team. They won't even know they're on it, just that we asked them out for coffee and then asked them a few questions.

No crest. Just coffee. This will be difficult at first because people use the phrase "We should get coffee" as conversational punctuation. They don't mean it most times, they just say it. You might have to ask a potential advocate to have coffee more than once.

■ What if You Don't Have a Single Advocate in Your Life?

First of all, you do. If we define advocate as "someone smarter than me," by pretending you don't know any possible advocates, you are saying you are the smartest person who ever lived. There's a chance you're not though, you probably didn't even know how deep the Mariana Trench was that I referenced in the first chapter or how much pressure it exerts on you (6.8 miles deep and 15,750 psi).

If you didn't know either of those facts, perhaps you're not the smartest person who ever lived. Perhaps the reason you don't have an advocate is that you just don't know where to look. That one's easy to fix.

Go where they go.

If you are an architect in a city that has more than one architect, you should be friends with that other guy. He might be a great potential advocate. You should join the local architecture chapter or group. You should make a goal to know one person at most of the firms in the city. Will you ever work at them? Maybe not, but I know you won't work at the one you are at forever. If there's not a group like that meeting where you live, all the better. Corner the market and start one. At the bare minimum, do this on online.

Maybe it's your job. You don't have the type of career that quickly lends itself to advocacy. You're an auto mechanic and the idea of rolling on your back on those amazing carts next to someone else to ask for career advice seems impossible. If you lived in Nashville, though, I know exactly where I'd point you—the Nashville Auto Diesel College. There is someone on that campus who is an expert. Even if they're not in the exact field you are, they have connections to other people who are. Does chasing them down sound awkward? Of course it does, but if you wanted to avoid awkwardness, you shouldn't have launched a Do Over. You should have launched a popover, which is a delicious, airy, pastry served with tea in the United Kingdom. They don't move your career forward but there's nothing awkward about the way those things hold jam and butter.

If you're an introvert and right now you're giggling at the odds of you ever doing any of this, let's start with something easier. Build a board of long-distance advocates. These can be authors, leaders or personal heroes of yours you might never meet. You'll never share coffee, perhaps, but their books and ideas can impact your career. I've never met him, but author Steven Pressfield greatly impacted the hustle investment of my Career Savings Account. I never would have been able to finish my first book without the encouragement of his book *The War of Art*. If advocates or a table of strangers feels like too big of a stretch, begin with a bookshelf.

■ Start with Two Questions

You called a possible mentor and they actually agreed to share coffee or a British pastry you're suddenly going to name drop like you're well traveled. Now what?

Ask them one of these two questions:

1. What is one piece of advice you'd give to a writer like me?

Or mechanic or whatever you are. You're not trying to exhaust the advocate with a "fix my entire career" conversation. Ease up on the nitrous, Vin Diesel. You're just trying to start a conversation, to ask a question that leads to places and this one does. I asked Adrian Zackheim what was the one piece of advice he'd give me during the writing of this book. He's the publisher at Portfolio. He's worked in the industry for thirty years and has published nonfiction legends like *Good to Great*. After some thought, he told me, "Remember, it's still about the book. In the midst of new opportunities and new options, it's easy to forget that it's still about creating a high-quality book. The book is still what matters most." To a young, prematurely gray-headed man like myself, that was really helpful. There's a lot of pressure on writers right now to be spread incredibly thin. You have to be speaking at events, and blogging and selling digital products and tweeting and building your brand, always building your brand. Most of the focus right now is put on promoting your book, not perfecting your craft. Adrian gave me the opposite advice. All because I asked him a question.

2. What did you wish you knew about work when you were my age?

Be careful how you frame this one, because you don't want it to sound like "Now that you're almost dead, what regret are you filled with that I need to avoid?" Try not to give your advocate a handful of calcium chews as you ask this one. The goal of this question is to spark some imagination for the other person, imagination born out of respect. You're saying, "You've got experience and wisdom I don't have, if you could go back in time and give the younger you advice, what would you say?" If the person you are talking to is younger than you, because you're new to a certain industry, edit the question. Instead, say, "What do you wish you knew about this industry when you were just getting started?"

Everyone has a cheat code. Ask them smart questions and you'll get smart answers.

▪ Allow Them to Ask Terrible Questions

Giving an advocate access means more than just opening up about our career, it also means opening up to questions. Not just normal questions either, but terrible questions. The kind of questions that will make you hate your advocate a little bit, sometimes. We have to give our advocates access to ask questions we might not want to answer at first or we'll never grow.

I was once stuck in a job. An advocate of mine asked me bluntly, "What's the story you want to be able to tell someday about this moment? What's the story that you want to tell your kids with this decision? That you played it safe, chose the easy route and never took any risks? Is that the story you want to tell?"

My first thought wasn't "I'm so glad I have an advocate! Hooray for probing questions!" My first thought was "I wish you'd shut up with your stupid questions coming out of your stupid face!"

On a different occasion, I told an advocate I was worried about a product I was launching. He asked me what my goal was. I told him "That the launch goes well and is great!" He said, "That's a terrible goal. How do you possibly measure that? How will you know you've succeeded? You're a perfectionist and the drug of choice for perfectionists is failure. If you never define the goal you can always fail. How many units are you going to sell by what date?"

Eventually I got over the audacity these advocates showed, trying to care about my career and challenging me to do the most with my life. The nerve. And I allowed their advice to challenge the decisions I was making about my Career Savings Account.

Letting advocates ask you questions not only helps you make the right decision, it also prevents you from making a terrible decision. People who can't be questioned often end up doing questionable things. Show me a leader who fell and I will show you someone without any advocates who are allowed to ask any real questions.

Remember

- A friend is someone you share your day with. An advocate is someone you shape your career with.

- Advocates must be brave, respected and trustworthy.

- Cheat codes make the game a lot easier and advocates will give them to you if you ask.

▪ The more access you give an advocate to your career, the more they can help you.

▪ Look for advocates who have industry, life or you expertise.

▪ Start advocate conversations with the two questions on pages 72–73 and allow them to ask you terrible questions in return.

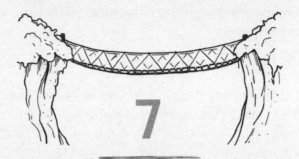

7

Don't Burn Many Bridges

It is seldom indeed that one parts on good terms,
because if one were on good terms one would not part.
—MARCEL PROUST

Don't burn any bridges is stupid advice.

Some people are not going to like you. There are people you work with right now who don't like you. There are people at your last job who don't like you. You don't control what other people think about you. Your Do Over might mean staying put at a job and improving it from the inside out. It could mean jumping jobs to another company. Stay or go, you'll have the opportunity to burn some bridges along the way.

I implore you, as someone with gasoline-soaked hands, do not burn many bridges.

Your industry is a lot smaller than you think. I don't care how big it feels right now, it's actually pretty small. You are going to continue to run into the same group of people over and over again. In a moment of frustration you will raise the gas can high. That attitude we talked about earlier in Chapter 2, will throw caution to the wind in reaction to a disrespectful boss, company or inanimate object like the printer.

Farewell foes, you say, throwing a match on a bridge you plan to never see again.

And yet, boomerangs return. Good ones and bad ones. The bridge you thought you were done with completely has a strange habit of coming back into the picture. You will work with some of the people you singed again. You will see them at industry events. They will be called by future employers for recommendations. They will be friends of other employers. You are not done with those relationships.

Some bridges need to be closed. They're toxic and harmful. You didn't light them on fire, you simply walked away from them and ended the relationship. But I swear, the fewer bridges you can burn in your career, the better your Career Savings Account will be. It's hard to build new relationships if you've got some old ones in the vault that are still smoldering.

▪ Even Stupid People Get Promoted

You don't like Brenda. She's not just a foe, she's your arch nemesis. Your Joker to Batman. You can't stand the way she laughs, she's not very good at her job and is a serial microwave popcorn burner.

It would be far easier to treat her with disdain. Perhaps not out-and-out disrespect, but it would be fun to talk behind her back. To join the "Brenda sucks" fan club, or if there's not one, form your own. You could be the president. Your mom always said you were destined for office!

But here's the problem: Brenda could be your boss someday. That might feel impossible right now. There's no way management would promote her. She's the worst! Can't they see that? Don't they know she's a credit thief, a meeting elongater, and so dumb she makes up words worse than "elongater" in her e-mails? They couldn't possibly make her your boss. And yet, that could happen.

I have seen far worse people than Brenda promoted. So have you. To argue otherwise is to believe that only amazing, noble, talented, kindhearted people hold positions of power at companies. Have you ever worked at a company for longer than seven minutes? Then you know that's not true.

I'm not going to address your attitude by trying to turn you into a nicer person more prone to help old ladies cross the street. I'm going to help you avoid burning the bridge with Brenda because even stupid people get promoted.

Next time you're in a meeting and you want to light some relationship on fire, I want you to say to yourself, "That person could be my boss someday."

■ Leave Jobs with One Finger Raised High: Your Thumb

When I left my first job at Details Communications, I left like they had deeply offended me. I drove home to Massachusetts and actually stopped at the border of Alabama to take photos commemorating my triumphant exit.

I embraced the new American Dream, I quit. I didn't just quit, I escaped! I broke free of the shackles of employment. Hurrah! Take that, day job!

The only problem is that Details was really kind to me. They actually gave me a good-bye lunch. And while I worked there, get this, they gave me a paycheck. Every two weeks. Like clockwork. They didn't trick me into the position either. I wasn't picked up off the street with a hood thrown over my head, shuffled into a dark van and spirited away to a cubicle.

But when I left with that attitude, I lit the bridge on fire.

You too will leave a job. That is going to happen. Maybe soon. When you do, make sure you leave with one finger raised high: your thumb. As in, "Thumbs-up guys, thanks for letting me work here. I'm off to a different adventure, but you guys are awesome." I know it's tempting to squeal out of the parking lot with a completely different finger raised, but that temporary good feeling you experience is not worth all the long-term relationships you lose by doing that.

I know that's easier said than done. There are some bad jobs out there with bad bosses and bad coffee. I'm not asking you to be fake and give long, deep hugs to people who spent the previous day verbally assaulting you. You don't need to make some wedding-level toast as you leave, thanking the academy for believing in your dream, mourning that you have to be whisked away from such an amazing environment.

Don't lie. Don't be fake. That's why it's just a thumb. One thumb up. The more you can do that, the more relationships you'll leave intact behind you and the less bitterness you'll bring with you.

■ Keep Your Matches Away from Digital Bridges Too

There are entire books that should be written on the subject of "don't be an idiot online," but since this isn't one, we'll just focus on the career ramifications of virtual tomfoolery.

If you currently have a job, do not go online and criticize the company you work for.

Your boss will see it.

If your boss doesn't see it, a coworker will. They will invite you to join the "We hate our jobs club" at your company, which is the worst club to join if you want a great career.

If your boss and coworker don't see it, other potential employers will. How do I know? Because you're going to get new job opportunities from places you least expect. Like casual relationships that follow you on Twitter.

No one sees your whining about your job and thinks, "We gotta get some of that at this company. The vitriol is off the charts!

Imagine what our team could do if we got a hold of that cancer!" Worst of all, digital bridges burn forever. Delete a tweet, remove a photo, it doesn't matter. The Internet never forgets and the fire you started will continue on some server you don't have access to.

If you have just left a job, don't do any social media gloating either. Don't passive-aggressively post photos about how you're so happy to be at a better job where people appreciate you. Don't engage in any sort of escape rhetoric. We all see through that. And it's insulting to the people who still work at that company you just left—people who don't think it's a hellhole. Your intention might be to criticize the last place you worked, but that criticism lands on the shoulders of anyone who is still there. You might not be saying, "I was smart to leave and anyone who stays at that company is a fool," but that is how it could be misinterpreted. Disagree? Sure, no one ever misinterprets statements other people make online.

■ What if You've Already Burned Some Bridges?

Leaving a job is an imperfect art form of which I have achieved finger-painting level. No matter how well you leave it, there are bound to be some hurt feelings, which again, you have no control over.

But what about the bridges you did burn? Through immaturity, arrogance or anger? What about the times you did indeed bow out with one finger raised but it was not the thumb? What then?

Apologize.

Not because it will perfectly repair the bridge. Not because you expect them to apologize in return for whatever wrong they did. Not with any expectation.

Apologize because it's the only way to get the soot off of your hands. It need not be complicated; in most cases an e-mail will suffice. I've written a few of those and they are never fun. I've sent handwritten notes as well, because they tend to mean more to people and they remove the pressure from the other person of feeling like they have to respond.

They don't.

One boss I apologized to forgave me.

One boss used my apologetic e-mail as a way to reply with additional criticisms.

I prefer the former, but neither response was really my goal.

An apology was. And I accomplished that.

Remember

- The fewer bridges you burn, the better your Career Savings Account will be in the long run.

- Your industry is smaller than you think. Treat everyone like you'll work with (or for) them again someday.

- Leave jobs with one finger raised high: your thumb.

- Don't be an idiot online. Digital bridges burn forever.

- Apologize when you should, repair what you can and leave behind what you must.

8

Community Shines Brightest in the Darkness of a Career Bump

We cannot help but tremble on the brink of surrender,
but it is our companions who give us the courage to jump.
—ALAN JONES

As we discussed, careers are not that complicated. There are only four general things that happen:

1. Career Ceilings

2. Career Jumps

3. Career Opportunities

4. Career Bumps

Relationships will play a role in all four, but they really shine when you experience a bump, something negative that happens to you that is out of your control.

In the Do Over chart, this season of career was the lower-left corner. A bump is when you get fired, you get laid off or you graduate into a difficult economy and can't find a job. It's an unexpected, undesired career transition that knocks you off your feet.

Who will be there to pick you back up?

Relationships.

In challenging moments in life, it will be friends and advocates who help pull us through. No one ever says, "When I hit rock bottom, my hustle was there for me." Instead, we tell stories of the friend who wouldn't let us believe we'd never have another job. We share tales of the neighbors who showed up when we needed them. We look back and wonder how money got in the mailbox when we needed it the most to get by. Your skills didn't put that envelope in the mailbox. Your relationships did.

We need relationships in these moments because there are really only two things that happen when we experience a career bump. We either break down or we break out.

■ For Some People, Rock Bottom Is a Trampoline

Having reached the breaking point, having hit some limit or wall in your life at the hands of someone else, you have something powerful in your hands. An invitation to reinvent your work.

You've heard this story a thousand times, in every part of life. This is the "I knew if I didn't stop drinking after that last job I lost, I would lose everything." This is the "When the housing bubble burst in Atlanta, I lost my job and had to start my career over!"

The crucible of brokenness has a funny way of leading to awesome lives. For some people, rock bottom is a trampoline. It springs them up from the depths, back into the light, fueled by a decision never to experience that low again. Or to help make sure other people don't end up there either.

Is there anyone who doubts that being fired from his own company didn't fuel Steve Jobs? Having lost his baby, having been pushed out by his own board in 1985, is there anyone who doesn't think he licked his wounds and started planning a triumphant return? Would Apple have been Apple without Steve's underdog moment that came full circle when he came back to Apple in 1996?[1] Hard to say, but his Career Bump did impact him and the company.

What's fascinating is that even the bumps that aren't work related can lead to new career adventures.

Jeremy Rochford's bump moment was getting kicked off a roller coaster.

One day he was at an amusement park with a group of friends. After waiting in a long line for a roller coaster, he was unable to buckle the seat belt for the ride. The manager of the park came over and told him not to worry, that they have extra-large seat belts. The guy running the ride said, "I've already tried the extra-large. This is the extra-large." The manager was so exasperated he kicked Jeremy off the ride and out of the park. He had to walk down a long line of laughing teenagers, the fat kid who was too big for the ride.

Years later, Jeremy is a personal trainer, author of a weight-loss book and two hundred pounds lighter. He couldn't have possibly predicted that getting kicked off a roller coaster as a teenager would become a defining career moment but it did.

The best part of all is that this isn't just motivational "get back on the horse" kind of nonsense. Scientists have been studying the impact of negative situations on creativity. They call it "posttraumatic growth" and have found five areas that show growth resulting from adversity:

Interpersonal relationships

The identification of new possibilities for one's life

Personal strength

Spirituality

Appreciation of life

In one study, Marie Forgeard, a researcher from the Department of Psychology at the University of Pennsylvania, even found that "the number of (adverse) events reported by participants predicted self-perceived creative growth as well as breadth of creativity."[2]

Why does this happen? Well, Scott Barry Hoffman, a psychologist at New York University, spent years studying creativity. He believes "a lot of people are able to use that (adversity) as the fuel they need to come up with a different perspective on reality. What's happened is that their view of the world as a safe place, or as a certain type of place, has been shattered at some point in their life, causing them to go on the periphery and see things in a new, fresh light, and that's very conducive to creativity."[3]

But not everybody loses the weight. Not everybody saves Apple. Not everyone says "Enough!" and dares to reinvent her career. We'd have a very different world if every negative situation bounced you automatically into a positive one. Many people, our friends, our family members and sometimes us, don't break out. We break down.

When you break down, you give up. You accept your fate. Who are you to dream? Fear gets loud in these moments offering complacency and bitterness as the only options. Having been beat up so often by the involuntary whims of life and others, we let go. We have not failed, we are failures. We'll never get a good job. We should just accept that work is a miserable thing and will always be miserable.

Having experienced a bump, we break down and throw our lot in with the 70% of Americans who are disengaged with work.

Unless, and this is a big unless, we have relationships.

The other investments in your Career Savings Account are helpful in these moments, but the one that will help you break out and not break down the most is relationships.

If you'll let them, Career Bumps offer you an amazing way to fast-forward and deepen the relationships you have in your life. Few things draw real friends like a crisis. (And if this isn't the perfect time to put your pride aside and ask for help from everyone you know including those boomerang relationships, I don't know when is.)

You will also discover something interesting here. When you experience a Career Bump moment, some of the friends you thought would be there for you will ghost. A portion of the people you thought would cheer will either disappear or in some cases flat-out oppose you. Other casual relationships you might not have connected with in years will come back into your life from the shadows to lock arms with you.

A Career Bump is like a sieve. Each relationship is like a marble in a bucket. When things are going well, you might not have a good sense of how strong or weak the relationships are. You don't really have to know because easy times don't test the strength of a relationship any more than calm seas test the strength of a boat. But a Career Bump turns the bucket upside down.

Suddenly, all the marbles fall into the sieve. Some relationships will fall through the holes, refusing to stick around for the messiness of a Do Over. Others, though, will get caught in the sieve, refusing to leave regardless of how large the holes in the sieve might be.

If you've spent time investing in relationships, the turnover of the bucket won't be nearly as dramatic. New opportunities won't take nearly as long since the first gig usually comes from relationships.

Our community makes it a lot easier for us to get back up, and in many cases will help us avoid falling in the first place.

I meet a lot of people who want to quit their jobs. I believe this is due to the fact that I wrote a book called *Quitter*. I am often their last bastion of conversation before they do something drastic like storm out of a company or launch a new business.

Regardless of the details and the specifics of their journey, I always ask the same question: "What is your team saying about all of this?"

More often than not, there isn't a team.

There's no handful of advocates or even a circle of friends carrying the weight of the decision with him/her. There's no group of people cheering the little wins or asking questions about the big plans. It's just one person staring out into a career void, feeling alone in a huge decision.

You're not meant to go it alone. Careers are best built in the context of community. A year into my last Do Over, I asked my wife one afternoon if I could go to the grocery store with her. I didn't need groceries, I needed company. I had so overfocused on the hustle part of my Do Over that I looked up and realized I was lonely. Jenny laughed that night about my desire to go see the butcher and the produce guy at Publix. Beware the temptation to isolate or hide during your Do Over. We need other people.

We need friends.

We need advocates.

We need relationships as a critical part of our Career Savings Account.

Investment 2
SKILLS

What you do.

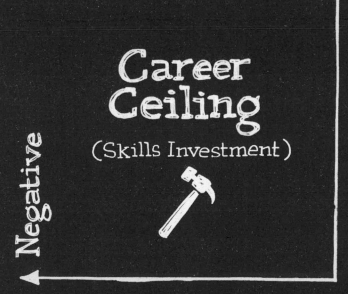

Voluntary

Career
Ceiling
(Skills Investment)

Negative

Investment 2: Skills

Everybody wants to be somebody: Nobody wants to grow.

—JOHANN WOLFGANG VON GOETHE

If your best friend was a horrible mechanic, you wouldn't ask him to fix your car a second time.

If your closest confidant was a terrible accountant, you wouldn't ask him to do your taxes.

If your lifelong buddy was terrifically irresponsible, you wouldn't ask him to watch your dog while you were out of town.

Would you still love him? Of course, you've got a strong relationship, but without better skills you'd never hire him again.

Relationships get you the first gig, skills get you the second. After who you know pays off, it's time for what you know to sink or swim. In extreme cases, if the skills portion of your Career Savings Account is dead empty, no amount of relationships is going to get your foot in the door.

When skilled, unknown writers ask me for a connection to a literary agent, I give them the name of mine. When unskilled, unknown writers ask me for a connection to a literary agent, I give them the name of my favorite book on how to become a better writer.

Skills are the bridge between amateur and expert. You know

who makes more money, gets more promotions and owns multiple belts, not the brown-on-one-side, black-on-the-other-side combo belt I own? Experts.

Want to be one? Work on your skills.

Skills also help give purpose to our hustle, providing guardrails around an otherwise exhausting source of energy that accomplishes nothing if it doesn't have a point. Hustle gets us running; having specific skills to focus on makes sure we're headed in the right direction.

Once you have skills, they are yours forever. No one can take that skill away from you. When you leave a job, the skills you learned there leave with you. You must keep them sharp, but a skill you put in the Career Savings Account stays there.

Skills are ability. Skills are natural talents you forced to go to the gym. They're unnatural talents you dug up through hard work and became better at. We often think they are stamped on our birth certificates at the hospital; you were either born a musician or not. But every bit of research argues otherwise. They can be learned. They can be grown. They can be changed.

When it comes to skills, old dogs can (and must) learn new skills.

And young dogs can save years of frustration by learning skills the right way to begin with.

In all this excitement and canine metaphor, let's not confuse confidence with skills. I love confidence, but I wouldn't want someone to confidence her way through a haircut. It's never your confidence I call into question when someone is around my head with a sharp pair of scissors. My college roommate once tried to save money by getting his hair cut at what I assume was an unaccredited, underground hair college. Emphasis on once.

He returned from this cost-saving exercise with hair that was long on the sides and short on the top. No one goes in and requests that look: "Trim my top down real low like I'm prematurely balding and then don't touch my sides, I'm growing those out." Skills matter.

In salon chairs and cubicles, they are critical.

If you have tons of character, hustle and relationships, but no skills, you become me in the NBA or Michael Jordan in baseball.*

In this section we'll discover why you already have more skills than you thought, how to master invisible skills, how to avoid becoming a dinosaur and how to find new skills. You'll also learn how skills are the key to getting unstuck. When you hit a Career Ceiling—the upper-left quadrant of our Do Over chart on page 13 representing a voluntary, negative transition—skills will be the hammer you use to break through.

*My apologies to Michael Jordan for using him twice as a bad example. He was very good at basketball. I'm not sure if you knew that.

9

You Have More Skills Than You Think

If we ever had coffee and I asked you what your skills are, after quoting Liam Neeson from the movie *Taken,* you'd probably tell me one of two things:

1. I don't know what my skills are.

2. I don't have (m)any.

The first answer might be born from the simple fact that you haven't thought about that question ever. I once had a job that required us to do self-evaluations of our own skills. This exercise felt like an invitation to invent new ways you were awesome. We were motivated to do this because we all knew our raises were dependent on it but we still had a hard time coming up with a list of skills. My coworkers and I would scratch our heads and write things like "numbers." My skills are numbers. That's not a skill, that's The Count from *Sesame Street*'s passion. That's a noun.

The second answer, the belief that you don't have many, is probably because you're human. We humans have a difficult job seeing our own skills as skills. Roy H. Williams, author and marketing expert, says, "It's hard to read the label when you're inside the bottle."[1] We don't consider them skills but rather just things we do.

So during this fictional coffee, the first thing I would do is to try to help you figure out what skills you already have. I'd even pull out a stack of note cards, which would probably make you recoil a little. Because once again, we're about to cross the threshold between dreaming and doing.

Dreaming is fun. Future results are enjoyable to talk about. Present efforts are not. But I'd push through all the hope you've stored in someday and try my best to get you to focus on the skills portion of your CSA today.

We tend to focus on "how to get more skills" first, which is understandable. "Get more" conversations invite you to dream. Assessing what you already have forces you to be honest. One of those is clearly more fun.

But this is a critical point in this section. Because now we're going to do some work.

The goal is to create a list of our current skills so that we know what we have to work with, what might be missing and what we want to improve. Don't worry—we won't be using note cards in the hustle or character sections—but when it comes to skills we need a method for figuring out where we are in order to head toward where we want to be.

We're going to build on the approach we started with in relationships. In that section, there was only one step: Write the name of someone you know who can help with your Do Over. Skills take a little more detail, but I assure you this is just as simple as the first exercise you already crushed.

▨ What We're About to Do

There are only two steps to this exercise:

1. Write down ideas.

2. Look for patterns.

For my high-detail friends this is like some sort of dream come true. You probably already have a note-card drawer sorted by color and size. For my low-detail friends, you are among company. I feel your lack of organization but I assure you that your career is worth it.

▨ Step 1: Write Down Ideas

I have a stack of cards on my desk.

One of them just says, "Naps." I have no idea what that means now. It's possible that at one point I was creating a list of things that are awesome or perhaps brainstorming activities Winnie the Pooh likes. Hard to say, but here's what's important: It doesn't matter.

I don't want your cards to be perfect. I just want you to write. I want you to work your way into the freedom to write down any skills that you like. I say work your way into it because like most people, you've been taught to be safe. Somewhere on the road to adulthood we decided that dreams were dumb. We stopped wanting to be firemen and astronauts and settled for stuck and predictable. We accepted the lie that Monday must be boring.

Step 1 is all about quantity. One skill per card, as many cards as you can come up with. This is not the time to edit. For now, we're going for volume. Don't ask yourself "Is this dumb?" It might be, and that's OK. All I want you to do is write one skill you currently have per card. Don't try to cram multiple ideas onto a single card.

To get started, here are some questions you can answer about your skills:

1. What are you good at?

Screw humility. This is no time to be humble. This is the hero's slow walk from an explosion moment. What's something you're good, dare I say, amazing at? Do you create great marketing proposals? Can no one balance a budget like you can? I'm not talking about just in your current job either. Go way back. If you were a fantastic paperboy, write down "On-time delivery." With relationships, we surfaced the casual ones because there's no telling where they might lead. Same with skills. Surface them all!

2. What comes naturally?

This question will generate some "Oh, this?" skills, those things you don't even think about because they come so naturally to you. You think everyone can do what you do, but we can't. The elaborate dinner parties you throw so easily, like Sarah and her Neighbor's Table, are indicative that you're amazing at event planning and connecting with others. That thing that comes naturally to you is difficult for the rest of the population. Just because it's easy doesn't mean it's not a skill.

3. What do people pay me to do?

If you've ever had a single job, this question is going to generate at least one note card. What were your responsibilities at your favorite job? Write them down, one card per skill. For instance, if you were in charge of quality assurance for software launches, write down, "quality assurance." Increase the cards this question generates by asking, "What skill would people pay me to do?" (Hint: The answer is "Almost anything.")

4. What are you afraid of?

Bears, obviously, but besides these furred denizens of death there are plenty of important skills hidden inside our fears. The reason is that great passions usually come with great fears. You've known you were supposed to do something for years, but have been avoiding it because you're afraid of it. Write that down. For example, I would list "writing" as one of my fears. Isn't that stupid to be afraid to do the thing I feel most called to do? It is, but no one ever accused fear of being smart. This one might feel counterintuitive because we're often told to answer the question "What do I love doing?" when it comes to figuring out our dreams and skills. I think that's an important question and one you could certainly ask with this exercise, but I've also learned we can be afraid of the things that really matter to us. Be honest with yourself. Do you really dread public speaking or are you afraid of it because you're worried you might not be good at it and it's something you secretly want to do?

5. If you wrote an eBook, what would the topic be?

Times are tough. Bills are due. Ma and Pa are about to lose the beet farm. The only way to save the situation is to write a twenty-page eBook that teaches eager shoppers to do something you're good at.

Are you renowned for your ability to pack ten days of clothes into a small carry-on for business trips? Have people marveled in the past at your skills in creating marketing strategies for book launches? Have you figured out a unique way to fit a fully functional wood shop in your garage but always thought of it as a silly hobby? If you had to create an eBook today, what would the topic be? If you had to write a series of three, what would be in your trilogy?

▓ Step 2: Look for Patterns

Now that you've got a few skills labeled you'll start to notice something: Some of the ideas are related. They might not say the same thing, but they are at least cousins in the family tree of creativity.

As you start to see some that are similar, begin grouping them together. Cluster them in a way that you can still see the nugget of each idea at a glance. If you create a vertical stack that covers up all the ideas except the one on top, you won't be able to see them all at once and might miss something important.

Group them in the way that works best for you. Maybe you want to group yours by "Skills I love doing," "Skills I get paid the most for," "Skills I want to improve" or "Skills I haven't used in a long time."

Don't worry if you don't come right out of the gate with some patterns. If this is your first go-round with an activity like this, you shouldn't be great at it yet. Try tweaking this exercise to make it work the best possible way for you.

Please don't get stuck using a tool that is designed to help you get unstuck. This shouldn't be a perfect process. In fact, I hope it's not. You should only spend a few minutes when you initially do this, then walk away. Building a Career Savings Account is a lifelong process; you've got time.

Put your cards in a spot where you will see them during your average day. I want you to bump into them as you walk to the kitchen or garage. Some (most) ideas are elusive. They don't walk into our heads and announce themselves; we have to capture them. And often they won't come out until they're positive we aren't trying to find them. Don't believe me? OK, so how come your best ideas come in the shower? Did you step into the shower and tell yourself, "Today I will condition my hair and try to brainstorm solutions to that problem at work"? Of course not. That wasn't even on your brain and yet, mid "repeat as necessary" the solution hits you!

I don't think you should bring waterproof note cards into your shower, but you should keep a stack of regular cards around. Fear would love to add the inconvenience of searching for one as a way to prevent an idea from seeing the light of day. Beat it back by keeping a stack in a few locations at home. And keep some in your pocket. It might feel a little strange, but anyone who judges you for writing down an idea and trying to be smarter about idea capture is a jerk. (You could always do this using an app on your phone but remember, there's still something powerful about physically writing an idea down.)

The goal of looking for patterns is greater clarity into what skills you possess. If you have ten skills written down, for instance, and nine of them fall into the category "Skills I don't use at my current job," we need to fix that. We need to find a new job that uses more of your skills, bring more of your skills to your current job or learn the skills your job actually requires.

If you ended up with two note cards and a pattern of "I have no skills, I hate you Jon Acuff," it might be time to phone a friend. Grab coffee with someone and ask them flat out, "What do you think my skills are?" If they're like my friends their first temptation will be to say something about your ability to pay "da billz," but immediately after they go to the extreme and rock a mic like a vandal they will surprise you with skills you forgot to write down.

This conversation will definitely help you, but it will also be excruciating. It will feel like you're asking a friend to list all of the ways you are awesome. Even if you set it up the right way and ask for a tangible skill and not a flowery compliment, you're still going to squirm while they respond. Suck it up. You're good at something. To pretend otherwise is a waste of time.

The point of the note-card exercise is to generate two different things:

1. Hope

2. Awareness

The first one is simple: Launching a Do Over takes a tremendous amount of hope. At the start of a journey like this, it's very easy to get discouraged and think you currently don't possess many career skills.

Hopefully seeing them on a handful of note cards for the first time has encouraged you that just like with your relationships, you're better off than you thought.

The second goal, awareness, is something that will also come up in greater detail in the hustle section. In the skills portion, the purpose of increased awareness is to help you see new skills you might want to acquire. Whether you want to get better at your current job or find a new one, chances are you will need new skills. Seeing what skills you currently have on note cards often helps increase the awareness of what's missing, those new skills you might need for a new job or to break through a Career Ceiling.

Remember

- Relationships get you the first gig, skills get you the second.

- You have more skills than you think. Writing them down and looking for patterns is a great way to discover that.

■ Don't let fear hide a skill you've always had or wanted to pursue. Just because you're afraid of doing something doesn't mean you shouldn't.

■ If you have a hard time filling out note cards, tag a friend in to help you.

10

Master the Invisible Skills

When it comes to work, most people define the word "skills" too narrowly. They assume it means "subject you have a degree in," or "stuff you can bullet point on a resume." Are those things skills? Certainly, but in order to reinvent your work, you'll need to reinvent your definition of the word "skills" first.

What's our new definition? Everything.

Everything is a skill.

Everything you do at work is a skill. Not just the abilities that show up in progress reports or HR files. Not just the actions that get you a nod of approval from a boss in a big meeting. Everything is a skill.

How you talk to people in the break room is a skill.

Your ability to fix paper jams in the printer is a skill.

Remembering a coworker's birthday is a skill.

Keeping your work vehicle clean is a skill.

Keeping your inbox under control is a skill.

Those might feel like tiny, insignificant things, but small skills have the tendency to add up to big careers. Think of it like compound interest. It's not sexy to slowly put away small amounts of money. But over time, the interest compounds and grows much larger than you'd think the sum of those investments would be. The same goes with those invisible skills we ignore most days.

They're not flashy. A lot of times they're not even fun, but if we ignore them, only focusing on the big, shiny, obvious skills, we miss a huge part of what it means to have a robust CSA.

And maybe you're like me. Reading about learning new skills and sharpening old skills feels a little intimidating at first. What if we could just tweak some things we're already doing every day? What if there are lots of skills we're already good at, that we could be great at if we just focused on them a little bit?

That's the power of invisible skills. They are easy and unseen, which means most people miss them. They ignore them and allow them to turn into weaknesses over time.

I wish someone had handed me this chapter the first seven years I was in the workforce. Every boss I had during that seven-year period wishes the same thing. I made the mistake of thinking you get a dream job when you graduate college. You don't. The goal of your first job is to teach you how to have a job. You don't know how to work when you graduate from college. You trade three months of summer vacation for eight days off a year. You don't think handling that transition takes some effort? You start attending meetings and working with people who might be difficult on projects that might last an entire year, not just a semester. There are so many little invisible skills to learn when you start working.

A lot of people will learn how to work in their first year or two. Me? It took seven years. I am a slow learner. I don't want you to be. Use me as a long-distance advocate with the ideas I'm about to share. So regardless of whether you've just entered the workforce or you've been working for fifteen years and have developed some bad habits, we need to shine a light on these invisible skills.

We'll start with the easiest because I'm generous like that.

▪ Go to Work

If you Google, "Why do people get fired?" you get a random collection of the most obvious advice you've ever read. One list mentioned that people often lose their jobs because they do drugs at work. That feels like something George Costanza would need to be told in an episode of *Seinfeld*: "Was that wrong? I gotta claim ignorance on this one. I was completely unaware that doing drugs at work was frowned upon."[1] You're smarter than George though, so I'll skip that pearl of wisdom.

What was revealing about the research into why people get fired is that one thing popped up on just about every list. It was the word "absenteeism."

Over and over again, career experts bemoaned the fact that employees who don't show up to work get fired.

So let's begin our walk through the invisible skills with the most obvious: Go to work.

Did you catch that one? Because it was fast and not very tweetable, let me say it again. Go to work.

If you're already doing that, then congratulations, you're one for one. That's a sweet feeling. Learning new skills. Sharpening old ones, that takes some dedicated hustle. But showing up for your job? Jackpot!

We can all do that one.

But someone isn't. Someone is taking too many dishonest sick days. Someone is coming in late. Someone is abusing the vacation policy. Someone is continually getting fired because they don't show up.

Don't be that someone.

Go to work.

Every day they expect you there.

Go on time. When asked what the best advice he ever received was, celebrity chef and CNN host Anthony Bourdain said, "Show up on time. It is the basis of everything."[2] Forget on time, show up a few minutes early. If you've worked at a company for all of four days, don't be ferociously insulted when they turn down your request for a weeklong vacation. If you get a thirty-minute lunch break, take a thirty-minute lunch break. If it's supposed to start at eleven, start it at eleven.

This feels insultingly simple, perhaps, but we have all worked with people who struggled mightily with everything in that last paragraph. You have a coworker who would find everything I just said revolutionary. Deep down there's a part of you that wants to photocopy this chapter and put it on their office chair but they'd have to actually be there to see it. I'm by no means advocating being the guy who shows up with the flu because he doesn't want to use a vacation day to be home sick. I can't stand that guy.

But if you want to start with an easy win, if you want to master the first invisible skill that a shockingly large amount of people miss, go to work.

■ Add Value

My brother is a lawyer. His job runs on the concept of billable hours. If he's not continually able to file billable hours that clients pay for, the partners at his firm will start to question why they hired him. It's an easy barometer of how he is adding value.

Most jobs don't have something as clear-cut as that, particularly a lot of white-collar jobs where nothing tangible is built. It feels more difficult to answer the question "Am I adding value?" but it doesn't have to be.

Every job has a currency. Whether you're working at a big corporation, a small start-up or chasing your own dream, there's a value system. Something that matters the most to that particular job. When I worked at the Home Depot, the currency of my position was writing compelling advertising, delivered on time, communicating what my boss wanted. If we were doing a catalog selling curtains, the currency that month was creating amazing copy about curtains and keeping the person who ran the curtain department happy.

If I did both of those things, I was adding value and my CSA was growing. When I tried to start an ad for granite with the headline, "Don't call it a comeback," I was playing to my personal currency of sneaking LL Cool J lyrics into things. I was promptly shot blocked by my boss.

If you've never asked yourself the question "Am I adding value?" start with an easier question. Ask instead, "What is the currency of my company?" If you worked at Southwest Airlines, one answer to that question might be "To provide a high-quality airline experience at a low cost." Then, once you've thought about that, ask: "What is the currency of my position?" That is, how does what I do every day add value to the overall currency of the company? If you were a flight attendant at Southwest, your currency might be delighting customers.

That's why when I flew with them to Las Vegas, they got on the intercom as we took off. At the airplane's sharpest incline, a flight attendant said, "We're headed to a party city so we're going to start the party early. She and her crew members then emptied large boxes of snacks into the air, the bags cascading through the aisles given our steep climb. People burst into laughter and shouts of joy as snacks flew through the air. It was an amazing moment that perfectly fit Southwest's currency of fun. Unless you have a peanut allergy, in that case it was your worst nightmare, bags of lightly salted death raining down on your face.

If these two questions (What is the currency of my position and the company?) feel insurmountable, do something crazy and ask your boss. Say, "I've been thinking a lot about the best ways for me to continually add value to this company. I'd love to hear your thoughts on how I can do that." Your boss won't answer, "No! You want to better serve this company? You monster!" More than likely they'll be thrilled you're trying to be a better employee.

The other reason I like asking this question is that it's the antidote to entitlement. For years I didn't ask "Am I adding value?" I asked, "How is this company adding value to me?" I had the relationship backward. I was demanding they improve my life and the minute they didn't, I fired up the bitterness machine.

You often see this when someone wants to go to a conference. They pick some vacation destination like Las Vegas or San Francisco. They ask the company to foot the bill for the flight, the conference and the hotel. When the company asks, "How will your attendance there translate to greater value for the department you work in?" the employee becomes indignant and just yells, "Vegas, baby!"

I once went to a conference in New Orleans. I stayed in the Ritz Carlton. My greatest takeaway from that experience was how to get my boss to say yes to things that were expensive and not that helpful to our company but fun for me to do. I wasted their money and I'm certainly not proud of that.

You'd never do that? You'd only go to conferences with clear, demonstrable, tangible value? You'd be the one who prepared a comprehensive explanation of ways you will use this newfound knowledge to become a better employee and submit that to your boss? See, you're winning again. I told you these invisible skills were easy!

If you don't have a job right now, go through the same exercise with the companies you are applying to. You might not be able to ask someone who works there, but you can ask the Internet with research. Your ability to match up your skills with the currency a company cares about most will help you stand out in the hiring process.

Employees who add value end up being invaluable. Work toward that.

■ Own Your Attitude

I've been fired before and I can say without a shadow of doubt it was a direct result of my attitude. I had a sense of entitlement, a mind-set that I was doing this company a favor by giving them my presence. I had the foolish belief that it was their job to fulfill my career desires. Shouldn't work be fun and life-giving all the time?

When that wasn't the case, I got bored, then I got frustrated, and then I got fired. That's usually how those things go. When you have a bad attitude it flavors every part of your performance. There's no visible or invisible skill that's safe from this particular poison. It has the potential to wreck your entire Career Savings Account. Entitlement hurts your hustle as well as your skill investment. The second you act like you've arrived, your willingness to work hard leaves.

Granted you completely changed your attitude in Chapter 2 when I encouraged you to, but for all those slackers, let me remind you of a few things:

Making sure you enjoy work isn't your company's job. It's your job.

Rescuing Monday isn't your company's job. It's your job.

Having a meaningful career isn't your company's job. It's your job.

We—not our company—are responsible for our attitudes. What happens each day at work doesn't get to determine my attitude, I do. Attitude is a decision. And it's a decision we have to make every day, sometimes every hour if that particular day is especially whack.

The best way to get a quick temperature check on your attitude is to ask a friend. (Are you noticing a pattern that relationships are important? Good!) And don't find your friend who has the worst attitude about their own job. They're going to say, "You've got a great attitude, you just work with a bunch of idiots!" Find the friend who's honest enough to say hard things. Better yet, find an advocate who can ask you terrible questions. When they give you good advice, be humble enough to actually take it.

Attitude is a skill. It can be changed. It can be improved and it starts with owning it. You determine your attitude, not your day, not a job, not a situation. You. Own it.

If you want a better job, start with a better attitude.

If you want a new job, start with a new attitude.

If you want to chase a dream, start with—well, "dreamy attitude" sounds pretty dumb when you type it out even if it's true.

Attitude impacts everything. Start there.

▨ Invisible Skills Black Belt

Already mastered the first three invisible skills? Champing at the bit for something more challenging than "go to work"? Great, here are nine far more obscure invisible skills I learned while spending fifteen years in offices and real-world examples of how to practice them.

1. Skill = Exceed Expectations

Real-World Example = If you need more to do, find more work to do. Finishing the work your boss thought would take you forty hours in only twenty-five hours doesn't mean you've just earned an extra fifteen hours of me time that week. A young lawyer I know makes a habit of asking partners in his firm if he can help them with their worst, messiest cases that they don't want to deal with anymore. The cases help him grow and let the partners know he's not afraid of hard work.

2. Skill = Be Diplomatic

Real-World Example = Don't park in the spot of the guy who is really serious about his parking spot. Or use the coffee mug of the lady who has a favorite coffee mug. Never engage in useless power struggles. Lose those battles on purpose and win the relationship instead.

3. Skill = Express Gratefulness

Real-World Example = Don't complain about the quality of the free lunch the company bought you. They bought you free lunch. Be grateful.

4. Skill = Show Consideration for Others

Real-World Example = Don't microwave seafood in the break room. Don't try to lie and say to people, "I brought in cod but it doesn't smell." It does. It's a creature from the black lagoon best served in restaurants that feature amazing slow motion butter montages, not break rooms. It smells.

5. Skill = Focus on What Matters

Real-World Example = Get obsessed about the quality of your work, not the quality of your title. One looks good for a business card, one looks good for your career.

6. Skill = Play to Your Strengths and Everyone Else's

Real-World Example = Don't schedule meetings that demand high creativity on Friday afternoon at 4:00 P.M. People are creatively empty then and their ideas will be too.

7. Skill = Be Flexible

Real-World Example = Don't constantly complain about the work conditions. (It's too bright, it's too dark, it's too cold, I wish it smelled more like cinnamon.) A simple rule of thumb to remember is, "Unless there's a live cobra in the office, I'll be all right."

8. Skill = Respect Their Gear

Real-World Example = Just because they gave you a phone, iPad or laptop, you do not now own a phone, iPad or laptop. Don't browse sites, install programs or download apps on there you wouldn't want to talk with your boss about.

9. Skill = Continue Your Education

Real-World Example = Make full use of any continuing education funds your company provides. Those are a dying resource and if your company wants to spend money to make you a better employee, jump all over that.

Every time you create a list of nine items instead of ten, an angel gets adult braces, but it had to be done. If you're OCD and need a tenth item to feel complete, here you go, "Don't print out a one hundred-page document and then abandon it, trusting that someone else will refill the paper tray when it inevitably runs out."

You'll notice that some skills seem to border on character traits. They're related because a skill well practiced and honed has the ability to become a character trait. The skill of being grateful, for instance, can become something automatic that you no longer have to think about with such a deliberate focus; you simply live it. That's why in the Do Over chart, skills and character are next to each other.

Regardless of how you approach improving your performance,

know this: Better employees get paid more, have better opportunities and chase better dreams.

Do these things and you will become a better employee.

Remember

■ Everything is a skill and can be mastered.

■ Go to work on time.

■ Add value to your job by understanding the currency that matters the most to your company, boss or industry.

■ Attitude is a skill too. If you want a better job, start with a better attitude.

11

Never Become a Dinosaur

I like being a beginner. I like the moment where I look
at everyone and say, "I have no idea how to do this,
let's figure it out."
—JUSTIN TIMBERLAKE

Based on the quote above, it looks like there are now at least two things Justin Timberlake and I don't have in common. I can't wear those tiny hats he brought back, and I don't love learning new skills.

I suppose there are other people out there like him.

They probably roll up their sleeves at the start of a new challenge, declare "Ballyhoo!" and then set right to work, smiling all the while and whistling a jaunty tune to help pass the day.

I am not one of these people, even though I keep running into people who remind me I should be.

In a period of thirty-six hours, I sat next to three very different people with three very different careers, who each told me how fast the workforce is changing.

The first was a pharmaceutical rep on a plane. He said that his whole industry was upside down. What concerned him most was that surgeons were starting companies on the side. I asked him what he meant, and he said, "They're the top of the food chain. For decades, if you made it there, you were set. If they're seeing the need to hustle on the side, what do they know that guys at my level don't know?"

The second person was a graphic designer who drove me back to the airport after a speaking engagement. He told me that when he was in college, digital design was an elective you could take if you wanted to but it wasn't important. Overnight though, it felt like if you weren't able to design online, you were a dinosaur. He said, "Projects used to go through an art director, a typesetter, a photographer, a graphic designer and a host of other people. Suddenly though, since your MacBook Pro could do most of those things you were expected to as well. It became the job of one designer."

The third person I met was a network engineer. He ran the network at a large company and said, "If I ignore where technology is headed for a month, I am out of date. Someday, a box of software is going to replace me and I'm trying to stay on top of that."

The speed of change is getting faster and faster. If we all don't want to become dinosaurs, bemoaning the good ol' days, we have to stay current. We have to stay relevant. We have to stay employable and the best way to do that is by learning new skills.

Instead of learning new skills, I like the ostrich approach where you just put your head in the ground and hope the rest of the world will somehow magically fix itself.

I tried that approach with a flight home from Los Angeles, though, and it didn't work that well. I hate details. Seeing details throws me into a bit of a panic. So I tend to skim instead of focus on them. For years I was able to get by with this approach because I worked at big companies where other talented people took care of most of the details. When I decided to work for myself, I was suddenly in charge of every tiny bit of information. My refusal to handle the details came to a head one day when I missed a flight.

On a Saturday morning, my wife called me when I was in Los Angeles. I was on a mountaintop, two hours from the airport. She asked, "Why aren't you flying yet?" I told her, "My flight doesn't leave until 2:45." She was quiet and then said, "So your expectation is that you leave Los Angeles at 2:45 P.M. Pacific time and land in Nashville at 4:45 P.M. Central time? What rip in the very fabric of time are you expecting Southwest to go through?" Cue wanting to throw up.

I had looked at my connecting flight time out of Dallas, not my starting flight time out of Los Angeles, which was 7:05 A.M. In my defense, I only missed the flight by a mere seven hours. So close.

Clearly I don't go into the dark night of a new skill willingly. I hang on to the edge of the old ones for dear life. Even as some new opportunity requires me to grow and develop different abilities, I bare my teeth and helicopter my fists like a child. I make loud, impassioned declarations about the foolishness of this new skill and bold claims about the excellence of the old way. It's not an old skill, it's a classic. This new one is a fad.

Were I born in another age, I would be the one on the side of the road brushing burrs off of my horse while the Model T whizzed by.

This is an unfortunate approach to take in life because new skills open the doors to so many wonderful things.

Like new jobs. New jobs always require learning new skills, even if that just means learning a different way a new company prefers to do something. They file their time sheets in a way you're not familiar with. Guess what, you have to learn a new skill.

New skills always lead to better resumes. Having Ruby on Rails on your resume if you're a developer will help you stand out in jobs that require Ruby on Rails skills. If you get them, that portion of the job market just opened up to you. If, on the other hand, you are confused why some lady named Ruby has a dangerous fascination with railroads, there's a chance you won't get that job.

New skills lead to better opportunities at the job you already have. "You know who we should fire, that guy who keeps learning how to do his job even better," said no one ever. Even before you've learned the new skill, just the act of signing up for class, wrestling with some new software or reading a book sends a signal flare to your boss that you care about your job.

Chasing a dream always requires learning new skills. I didn't get to be a public speaker by not speaking publicly. I had to learn that skill. I didn't know how to travel very well. I'd never done even really simple things like renting a car by myself. If you try to tell me that driving over those spikes at the rental car return at the airport is not horrific, you are a liar. (I know, look at me doing things now like renting cars all by my big self now that I'm self-employed!) There are about one thousand new skills I get to learn as I chase my dream.

The flipside is true, too. Learning a new skill can reveal a new dream. How can you know you love doing something if you don't try it? The popular approach to figuring out a calling is akin to sitting in a cabin in the woods and waiting for the calling to show up. That's ridiculous. Passion is often found in the crucible of work. Sometimes you have to get your hands dirty before you can know what your passion is. Alex Atala would tell you that, if you ate at his São Paulo restaurant D.O.M., which is number 7 on the S. Pellegrino list of the World's 50 Best Restaurants.

Time magazine put him on the cover and labeled him the "God of Food." Surely, someone with such a deep, rich Career Savings Account knew all along he was meant to be a chef? Nope. "Atala found his calling while scrounging for money as he backpacked from nightclub to nightclub in cities from Berlin to Milan." He never had designs to be one of the world's greatest chefs. "He started working in kitchens because it was a job a Brazilian in Europe could get. He discovered he was pretty good with a knife."[1]

Learning something new always leads somewhere new. It has to, that's the very nature of new. You don't learn something new and end up somewhere old.

Bottom line: If you want a new job, better job, or your dream job, you need to learn new skills.

If we know it's the best thing we can do for our careers, why don't we do it? Because it's also the worst.

▓ The Many, Many Hassles with Learning Something New

For starters, you look like an amateur. This is not a threat, this is a promise. Whenever you learn something new, you look like an amateur because you are. When people who live in Cleveland, Ohio, visit Paris, France, they look like tourists. That's OK. They are tourists. That's how they should look. You don't have to wear a fanny pack, no one does really, but you wouldn't beat yourself up for not having intricate knowledge of the city. You'd get lost. Even with a smartphone, you'd end up in Rue de something. You'd go to all the tourist spots like the Eiffel Tower and do all the things tourists do. Because you've never been there before. For some reason we're afraid to be tourists when we start new skills, which is a shame because it's a great approach.

Think about it, what do tourists have in common? They ask lots of questions. They don't pretend to be something they're not. They don't feel the pressure to know everything. They give themselves permission to be excited about experiencing new things. And they have fun! It's not easy to learn something new but approaching it like a tourist makes it a lot easier.

The other problem with learning a new skill is that it takes forever. How long is forever exactly? Longer than you thought. We tend to set impossibly short timelines to learn new skills. "Entire new language you want me to program in? Cool, should have that done by this afternoon." When it takes longer than that, and it will, because getting good at anything does, we get mad at our lack of progress.

It also seems like everyone around us is faster at learning new skills. Isn't that annoying? That guy who wrote that new book? Probably took him fifteen minutes. That woman who just got promoted because of her tech savvy? It took her a long weekend to develop that complete toolbox of awesomeness.

It doesn't feel good to learn something new either. The after is amazing. Doing something challenging and then looking back on what you were able to do is fantastic. That's like a commercial for Diet Coke. The during, though? That can be miserable. Not just because we're lazy either, but because our brains conspire against us. They have well-worn neural pathways that make the old way of doing things feel better. It's more familiar. The actions we take are more automatic. We get to go with the flow. Studies into our bad habits have even revealed that "the brain sets up defense mechanisms to prevent you from changing what is automatic and unconscious."[2] We are propelled down the stream by months, if not years, of momentum.

Learning a new skill is not fun, but it is important and it is possible. That same brain that worked against you can work with you thanks to neuroplasticity. Your brain is continually growing and changing; that's not something that stops in adolescence. "Every time you have a new thought, you are creating new pathways in your brain. And every time you have the same thought, or recall a memory, you make that pathway stronger and more dense."[3]

If we can change our brains, we can certainly reinvent our work, but we have to learn new skills.

If you want to have a Do Over, you have to do that. A lot. Regularly. Constantly, at times.

So it appears we're at odds. It's critical, but miserable. The best worst thing. The solution is to stop fighting the need to learn new skills. Ignoring the need doesn't make it go away either. It just turns us into dinosaurs that can't catch planes. We need to find a way to rig the odds in our favor. The house doesn't always have to win if in the next chapter we look for new skills in the last place you'd expect.

Your past.

Remember

- Your career will become extinct unless you learn new skills.

- If you want to learn a new skill, give yourself permission to be a tourist, not an instant expert.

- New skills make you "stuck proof." It's hard to get stuck in an old situation when you put a priority on investing in new skills.

12

Win the Way You Won Before

You have learned a new skill in the past.

Don't think so?

OK, you probably know how to drive a car.

No? I bet you can ride a bike.

Still no? I bet you can tie your shoes.

Three strikes? Really? How did you get this book? Who gave it to you? Was the Do Over they were hoping you'd embrace you getting rid of your Velcro shoes since you refuse to learn how to tie laces? So many questions.

The reality is that we've all learned how to do something new in the past. (You learned to read, for instance.) We're not starting at zero. The skills portion of your Career Savings Account is not empty despite what fear and doubt might be telling you right now. You've won before and now we're going to win that way again.

▪ What Skill Did You Learn in the Past?

It'd be awesome if your reference point is career related, but it doesn't have to be. Perhaps quitting smoking was one of your greatest wins and holds the key to the next one. You get to choose it, not me.

Have you ever gotten a promotion? Did a manager make a point of recognizing you in a meeting for something great you did? Did you lose fifty pounds? Did you complete a project the rest of the team thought was impossible? Somewhere in your history is a win. Go find it. I'll wait. Got it? Jot it down in the margin of this page.

▨ Why Did It Work?

That thing you succeeded at, why did it work for you? What were the circumstances that conspired in your favor?

Maybe you were motivated by a deadline. Knowing that your boss was expecting the report by Monday morning drove you to work hard over the weekend. (I always thought the whole "I want this on my desk by 8 A.M., Johnson!" was just something that bosses said in movies. Nope, that happens in real life, too.) Without a deadline you would have floated along on the project taking weeks to complete it. Maybe the pressure of that due date gave you fuel to push through the fear of learning something new. If that's the case, you're going to need a deadline with this new skill, too.

Perhaps you had an audience that drove the development of your new skill. Being on stage and running out of material before my speech is supposed to be over really motivated me to get better at public speaking. I started timing my speeches and practicing them because I knew an audience would be present when I actually gave my presentation. Was there some positive peer pressure that kept you going? If so, you better find a new audience for this new skill. It doesn't have to be a crowd unless it was a crowd before. If you learned some skill in the past because your old boss asked you to give a presentation on it, go find a new crowd to share the new skill with.

Was there something completely ridiculous that helped you

learn the skill? Did you have to come up with some silly reward system? If you practiced guitar for a solid week, you'd give yourself a treat at the end. That sounds like you got a milk bone but if you're a guitar-playing dog reading this book right now, there are bigger forces at play. Was there a reward involved? A consequence? A mantra? A note card? Some sort of game?

I'm personally motivated by countdowns. Over the years, whenever I've needed to do something I'm afraid of or find difficult, I set the timer on my phone to 60 minutes. I figure I can do anything for that short length of time. What I've found is that once I've started, it's a lot easier to continue. Sixty minutes often turns into 120 minutes, which turns into 180 minutes as I gain momentum. The timer trick helps me "break the ice" of the task at hand, so to speak.

To work through the edits of this book, all four hundred of them, I decided to win the way I'd won before. Since it was a big task, instead of sixty minutes I wrote down one hundred hours at the top of a piece of notebook paper. I knew it might take more time than that, and it did, but it gave me a place to start. Every time I spent hours editing the book I counted them down. Day by day over a three-month period I marked down my hours. By the end of it I was really excited to get to zero. Is that silly? Of course it is, but it worked. Don't be afraid to be ridiculous in the pursuit of new skills.

The goal of interviewing an old win is to drag forward what worked in the past into the present so you have a great future. Of course, you can't photocopy the past and expect it to work in an entirely new setting. My ability to braid a horse's tail probably would not have served me well in learning the new skill of driving a Model T. It's not about repeating the past, it's about learning from it and setting yourself up for the greatest chance at success. Which is why I took a sixty-minute trick that had worked before and created a one-hundred-hour version to help me finish this book.

You've done this before. You've got a win somewhere in your history. If you want to have one in your future, too, stack the odds in your favor by bringing in all the heavy hitters.

Deadlines.

Audiences.

Checklists.

You need a lot of new skills to get where you're headed but you're already much better at learning new skills than you want to admit.

Remember

- If you want to win in the future, sometimes you have to look to the past.

- Interview a former win. Why did it work? What about that situation made it more successful than others?

- Never reinvent the wheel. What can you do today to help re-create some of the circumstances that helped you win yesterday?

13

Kick-Start Your New Skills
with Something Fun

So, friends, every day do something that won't compute.
—WENDELL BERRY

We need new skills because they lead to new jobs, new dreams and new opportunities. We've won before and we're ready to win again.

Now, what's one new skill we want to learn?

There are two easy ways to pick one: by necessity or curiosity.

Necessity, in addition to being the mother of all invention, is also the origin of a lot of new skills. The graphic designer we discussed in chapter 11 was learning new skills because his livelihood is dependent on that. That's what we call a "should skill," as in, "I should do this if I want to have money for things like pants and apples." I too am a fan of both of those things.

Curiosity is just the opposite. It's a skill born out of desire. It's something you're interested in trying. Maybe you've thought about doing it for years but never had the courage. Perhaps it's a new hope you've only had for a few weeks. It's not a should skill, it's a "could skill," as in, "You mean I could spend time learning that? Really? Me?" This is also what grandmothers who want another cookie say in the South to disguise their true feelings: "Oh I couldn't."

Both types of skills are important to our careers, but we're going to start with one from the curiosity side of things. You already have a long list of shoulds in your life. I should exercise more. I should watch what I eat. I should not get so mad during my commute. Even as we talked about new skills related to your job, you probably thought about a few that you should be learning.

At the heart of this book is the belief that work doesn't have to be miserable. We can rescue Monday and do meaningful work if we build meaningful Career Savings Accounts. As we survey our lives for a new skill to add to our accounts, if we grew up with the broken belief that work is bad, we'll be tempted to pick a new skill that perpetuates that belief.

When I challenged readers of my blog to learn a new skill, the one I picked for myself was e-mail marketing. I hated it. It was like eating raw turnips. I knew I should do it but it was miserable. I messed it up countless ways and ended up getting in mild Internet trouble because of spam. I wasn't doing anything nefarious; I'm not smart enough to even know how to spam. But hundreds of people reported me as spam because I was clueless. This new skill exercise left me tired, frustrated and eager to focus on playing the Plants vs. Zombie app. Why did I choose e-mail marketing right out of the gate? Why will you pick the same thing if you're not careful? Because if you learned that work is meant to be tedious, you'll pick new skills that fit that M.O., too.

I'd rather us take a smarter approach and start with something fun and easy, a curiosity skill. I want us to have the greatest chance of success because if we can learn one small skill, it can create momentum for one slightly larger skill. Let's get an easy win right out of the gate and build on it. Winning at a curiosity skill first can give you the energy to take on a necessity skill next.

There will be plenty of time in life for should. Right now, let's figure out a could. If you could add any small skill to your career, what would it be?

▪ Keep It Simple

Most of the time, learning something new requires five different things: time, gear, money, access to experts and knowledge.

For our purposes we're going to only focus on two of those: time and knowledge. If you shoot for all five, you create obstacles between you and the skill.

Let's imagine you are an art teacher at a high school. You want to add a new skill to your CSA to increase your job security and give you access to more jobs. You've always thought about trying pottery.

If you focus on the wrong aspect of pottery, that would be a difficult skill to start with because it's not cheap. You'd need access to experts, which costs money. You'd need to sign up for a class, which would cost money. You wouldn't have much control over the class schedule either. You couldn't practice it at home unless you got your own wheel, and even then you have to do that whole scene from the movie *Ghost,* which is super messy and awkward. You'd need to pay for materials like clay and the rights to the Everly Brothers' song. This is already feeling like a huge hassle. Better quit for now. Maybe you can learn something new later. Like next year. Or never.

To prevent these feelings, we're going to break that seemingly large, obstacle-laden skill of "pottery" into smaller pieces. We're going to find the little skills hidden inside the big. Instead of focusing on the expensive and complicated aspects of pottery—gear, money and experts—we're going to focus on the aspects we have instant access to: time and knowledge.

The latter is easy, they have free knowledge available at the library and this other thing I've been hearing a lot about: the Internet. Just gaining knowledge might not feel like enough effort at first, but remember, this is the beginning of the skill, not the completion. We're so eager to get to kiln level that we rush right by "Reading a book about pottery" or "Visiting antique stores and sketching shapes of pots that inspire you." Both those activities are fun, free and easy.

What about time, though? We need that because if you want to get better at something, it always costs time. If you don't have any, steal some from *The Bachelor*. Or Facebook or any number of things that are requesting that resource without paying you anything in return.

■ When Are You Going to Work on This Skill?

Most of us will work on our skills eventually. Ask anyone who has been caught off guard by a Career Bump and they will tell you they thought they'd have more time. But life is busy. Learning a new skill, honing an old one, both of those things are fairly quiet. They don't loudly demand time from us, so we tend to believe we will work on them eventually. That's why you see bald tires on expensive cars.

The owner of that vehicle probably has the money for new tires. They have the head knowledge that you should be able to cover Abe Lincoln's head on a penny in the tread as a simple test to see if they are still good. They might even have purchased that car because of its many, many safety features.

But they don't replace their tires because they got too busy or they didn't notice. They didn't own the when. (That felt like a line from the movie *Pocahontas*.)

We're going to, though, since time is the biggest cost we're going to be paying our new skill.

If you really want to learn something, you have to decide when you are going to do it. Otherwise, you dramatically reduce your odds of actually doing it.

There are two ways we need to look at when:

1. Macro

2. Micro

Let's talk macro. This is the act of taking a broad look at what's ahead in the next month. I do this by printing out my calendar for the month. I also have a huge yearlong calendar I've mounted on a foam board in my office. Macro means large scale, so that's how I approach it. Doing this allows you to see how soon something is really due. Christmas always feels far away until a store tells you, "Only nineteen more shopping days." Reframing the information gives you new insight and allows you to ask important questions such as:

How much time do I really have available in the next month?

Are there insignificant things vying for my time that I need to cancel?

Is the year shaped in a way that offers me the greatest chance at success or do I need to adjust my expectations given the other things I've already committed to?

The funny thing about taking a macro look at your time is that it always reveals two conflicting truths:

You have more time than you think.

You have less time than you think.

The first one happens because fear tells you that you don't have enough time. You're too old, you're too busy and you've missed your window. A professor at Frostburg State University in Maryland told me she felt ancient when she went back to get her master's degree. I asked her how old she was at the time and she replied, "Twenty-nine!" Now in her late forties, she laughs at what she used to define as "old."

I'm convinced that fear beats the "You don't have enough time" drum because it never wants you to invest in your career. It always tells us we don't have enough time to be the people we've always felt called to be. This is a lie and seeing your whole calendar in a macro way will reveal it as such as you realize how much time is actually in an entire month or an entire year.

At the same time, you'll realize that you have less time than you think. Once you add commitments and weekends and vacations and all the legitimate things that take calendar space you'll feel there's less time than you thought. Don't be discouraged by this. By seeing what's coming you can get ahead of it; a realistic calendar view helps you prevent holding yourself to gruelingly large expectations.

You can also plan backward from the due date. If you picked learning a particular compliance procedure as your skill because you would like to do a presentation using it on August 13, start there. Place a big red "X" on August 13 and then plan backward. What will you need to accomplish in the weeks before that date to make sure you're ready?

Next, we look at the micro. This is simply figuring out what specific times and specific days you will work on your skill. The more consistent you can be with your time, the easier it is to get the clock to work with you and not against you. Your day is too busy to leave things that are important to you up to chance.

The two best ways I know to find time during a single day are to be honest about where my time is going and to start with what matters first. When it comes to managing our time on a micro level most of us are like dieters who want to lose weight but eat meals with blindfolds on. We have no idea where our time is really going. Since this is a career book, instead of asking you what calories you're consuming daily, I'll ask you: What's consuming your calendar daily?

I thought I was really busy one fall while speaking at a dozen events but I somehow managed to power watch an entire season of a show called *Blacklist* on Netflix. In one week I was able to watch twenty-two episodes of a forty-five-minute show, all the while bemoaning how swamped I was. Worst of all, I committed Netflix adultery, leaving my wife behind in the series as I galloped ahead without her. Turns out I am less busy than I thought and you might be, too. Be honest about your day; where are your hours going?

The second approach to managing your time is to start with what matters most. I've made night owls my enemy with the previous books I've written because I advocate getting up early. I'll spare you an additional lecture on the merits of rising early. Let's say you like to sleep in most days. My 5 A.M. is your 8 A.M., perhaps. That's fine, just promise me you'll start your day with what matters most.

Days are like snowballs rolling down a hill. I don't care how perfectly you've planned it, something unexpected is going to get picked up as your day rolls down the slope. A client you weren't expecting will call. An emergency will pop up. A last-minute meeting will be scheduled. By the end of the average day, the snowball will be covered in things you couldn't have anticipated when you first rolled it down the hill that morning. If you've got something important to do, find a way to do it first, before the unexpected happens.

■ Who Will Help You Learn This New Skill?

Part of what's fun about the Career Savings Account is that all the pieces work in concert. And we're discussing them in a certain order on purpose. We started with relationships because each subsequent investment will require people who help us. Skills is certainly no exception.

Who is going to help you learn this new skill? This isn't about access to experts, this is about access to friends. It's easier to learn a new skill when you have someone helping you. Most of us love the one-man wolf-pack mentality. It's us against the world! We're going to do this alone. Garbage.

Big dreams take other people. So do small skills.

So who is your who?

Who is going to call you on your excuses?

Who is going to celebrate your successes?

Who is going to track the progress with you?

They don't have to be a best friend, spouse or lifelong companion. Don't put that pressure on yourself. Your who could just be someone you check in with via text every few days. I would argue that the person who fits this position will probably come from the casual friend category of your relationships. An advocate could as well, but since we have so few of those, don't be afraid to ask a friend. Look through your relationship note cards to find someone.

Here's a warning: On some days, you're going to hate this person a little bit. During the moments that you want to be lazy and coast, they are going to reach out to you and ask how things are going. You are going to want to ignore them or be curt. If you've ever had a personal trainer, you know this is true. We love to say we're going to change but when someone pushes us past our comfort zone sometimes we get frustrated. That's OK. But keep going.

An accountability partner you only contact when you are winning isn't an accountability partner, it's a cheerleader.

It's also important to set expectations. Don't tell someone, "Hey, I need you to check in with me every day for the next year." Especially if the person you are talking with is a casual friend. Don't overwhelm someone or give them a thousand words explaining your goal if they're a low-detail kind of person. Communicate in the language they speak.

I've had the greatest luck with checking in with friends twice a week, once on Monday and once on Thursday. I also found that my success rate dropped significantly depending on how busy the person was. The temptation is to find someone else who is grinding on a project, someone whose current effort in their own life inspires you. That's not a terrible thing, but just understand that busy people are, well, busy.

In some rare cases, you might not even need to know your "who." I was once really motivated by a guy who tended to work out at the gym at the same time I did. This is going to make me sound a little like a lunatic, but I always tried to run longer than him on the treadmill or lift more than him on the days our exercises overlapped. Maybe if your new skill is promptness, which allows you to get to work before most other people, your who is the woman who keeps beating you there. You might never actually talk to her about the skill you're working on but she still keeps you going. If that seems dumb, please go on Pinterest and count the number of boards people have dedicated to photos of in-shape strangers who inspire them. And then write me an apology card.

I still think it's best to have your who be someone you are actually in a relationship with. But let's not pretend that's always easy. I hate when books tell me, "Without a deep heart friend this next task will be impossible. Choose someone from your fifty best friends. La, la, la." Having a friend to walk this road with you makes it easier but if you can't think of a single person, try the skill anyway. Sometimes you have to start learning the new skill first before a boomerang friend shows back up to help you. It's amazing how posting something simple on Facebook like "I'm thinking about learning _____, does anyone have any experience with that?" can boomerang people back into your life.

Learning a new skill doesn't have to be miserable, especially if you start with something fun and easy. How will you know when you've found the right curiosity skill to learn? When it feels like it "doesn't count."

Want to strengthen your vocabulary? Don't buy a boring book on "power words," subscribe to *The New Yorker* and read only your favorite section. That counts.

Feel like you want to meet more people outside of your industry? Take your skill of cycling and join a cycling club. That counts.

Curious about becoming a better public speaker? Go to a local comedy club on Open Mic Night or even take an improv class. That counts.

We're so conditioned to believe that learning something new has to be like eating a vegetable that when someone hands us a piece of fruit we're apprehensive. Are you sure this counts? Are you sure something enjoyable can move me forward in my career? Are you sure a Do Over can be fun?

I am.

Remember

- There are two ways to pick a new skill to learn: necessity and curiosity. Picking one based on curiosity at the beginning of a Do Over is the easiest way to create momentum.

- Learning a new skill requires five things: time, gear, money, access to experts and knowledge. Start with the cheapest first: time and knowledge.

▪ Look at your time in two different ways: macro and micro. Macro gives you a look at your month and year. Micro gives you a look at your day.

▪ Big dreams take other people. So does learning something new. Find someone from your relationship note cards to help you.

14

Skills Get Sharp Slowly
and Dull Quickly

New skills and old skills have one thing in common: they both go dull if you don't use them.

If you don't sharpen them, they're useless. More than that, they get a little scary because in the absence of use, fear takes root.

My greatest skill is writing.

Every day that I choose not to write is like a sapling falling into my garden.

If I miss a day or two among the rows, that tiny tree doesn't have much time to grow. When courage or curiosity takes me back to the keyboard, I am able to pull it up from the ground easily. I am not afraid I'm not a good writer anymore, it's only been forty-eight hours. The skill has barely dulled. But every day I refuse to put in the work, the roots grow deeper.

After a week of not writing, I can no longer jump back in easily. It takes both hands for me to pull up the sapling of fear out of my garden.

After a month, I need a shovel.

After six months, a backhoe.

Now I can't casually stroll back into the garden. I need to psych myself up first. I need to get tremendous encouragement from friends. I need to find someplace that rents metaphorical farm equipment. There are now a lot more obstacles standing between me and sharpening this skill.

The tree is deep now. I'm not just afraid of using the skills I've ignored, I'm ashamed. I know I should have started earlier, not to let the skill go quiet. Not to let the fear burrow down and establish roots. But I did, life got busy and every day I didn't write, it got easier to believe I was not a writer.

It's hard to sharpen your skills, but I have some wonderful news.

Today is the easiest day you'll ever get to. Today the roots of fear are the smallest you'll ever face. You have more time left in your life today than you will ever have again.

To the garden we must go!

■ The Hardest Competition You'll Ever Face

I've never played in the NFL. That might surprise you, since most peoples' reaction upon first meeting me is, "I bet he played professional football," but it's true.

I never played football growing up, content to play soccer instead, given my "flier" body type. I didn't know what "flier" meant until I heard a professional wrestler describe two other thin wrestlers that way. He meant they were light and able to do a lot of acrobatic top rope moves. That sounds way cooler than "skinny." So going forward, please refer to me that way.

Despite my lack of football experience I once got to speak at an event with two other professional football players. One was a quarterback named Rusty Smith and the other was a safety named Bernard Pollard.

The average career in the NFL is fairly brief. The union claims it's 3.2 years; the NFL claims it's about 6 years.[1] Either way, that's not long. Talk about a Do Over, imagine the career you've been working your entire life toward, from Peewee football to college, is over after 6 years and you're 27 years old? You still have 50 odd years of life expectancy and have to come up with a new career!

At the time we spoke, Pollard was starting his ninth year as a player, which makes him unique.

I asked him what the unexpected secret is to having a long career in the NFL.

Without missing a beat he replied, "The secret is that you have to outsmart yourself. You have to get your routine. You have to get your system together as a player. The things you always do. Off-season, during the season, you have to have your list. That's why every week I know which days I'm going to be doing weight work, cardio, sauna, ice bath, etc. I take care of my body. Some guys can't handle the mental discipline of it, especially once they've made some money."

You probably won't play in the NFL. If this book helps you do that, please tweet me at @JonAcuff. But what Pollard said about playing football longer than most people is true for ensuring your Do Over has a longer shelf life than the average New Year's resolution, too.

Sharpening skills is about learning to outsmart yourself, which means dealing with our "first times."

▨ The Problem with First Times

The first time you do anything should be the hardest time you ever have doing it.

Think about the first time your dad tried to teach you how to drive a stick shift. You ground the gears, you stalled out at the slightest hill, and you bucked that car back and forth, much to your father's chagrin.

You were horrible at driving a stick shift.

Why?

Because it was your first time.

Think about the first time you tried to use a new project management system at a new job.

You were a pro at stuff like that at your last job. You could comment on projects and track work with the greatest of ease. But then you changed jobs. Their system was different from the last system you used. It was awkward and time consuming. You kept sheepishly asking coworkers the simplest of questions. Six months later, you don't think much about it; what was once a confusing system is now second nature to you.

It's not just work or tasks where we see this happen, either. For years, I've used iPhones and iPads. One Christmas, my bookworm daughter got a Kindle. I'd never used one. I immediately picked it up and tried to swipe things as if it were an iPad. None of the flow was the same, the user experience was completely different and it was frustrating. I felt like a caveman banging on it with a rock trying to find the book that was hidden inside.

First times should be the worst times when it comes to learning something new.

And the reason we have such a hard time outsmarting ourselves and sharpening our skills is hidden in this point.

When it comes to our careers, most of us make every time the first time.

Call it a casualty of speed or just a lack of self-awareness, we often approach every single task and opportunity like it's the first time.

Disagree if you must, but if you're a business traveler, please go pull out the list you created of the items you always pack for every trip.

I don't mean the list in your head, that thing is unreliable and likely to get distracted by an amazing cat video on the Internet. I mean the physical, or digital, list of items you always pack.

You probably don't have one. I've flown around three hundred times in the last two years, spread out on different airlines to make sure I never acquired any sort of status, and I didn't have one at first.

The night before every flight, I would essentially sit down and say to myself, "Let's act like this is the first time I've ever flown to a speaking event! That's the best way to make sure I didn't learn anything from last time and can make this experience as miserable as it can possibly be!"

Then I'd throw a bunch of things together, inevitably forgetting something that matters. I have bought running shorts in most major cities. And a tie a time or two. You do this, too. Maybe not with packing, but with something else in your life. You make every time the first time, and you never bother to learn from the last time.

That's what sharpening a skill is, learning something new and then building on what you learned. Each repetition is like laying another brick on the foundation; you get higher and higher. But most of us never stack the bricks. We start each foundation like it's new, never progressing.

This is bigger than just skills. We act like every new job we get is completely new. It's not. There are great skills you learned at the last job that you need to unpack at the next one. That's why we focused in Chapter 12 on winning the way we've won before. (There are also bad habits you need to leave behind.)

What if we could pay attention the first few times we did something? What if we could pay the upfront cost of effort at the beginning of a skill? That's why we don't learn, it feels like too much work at first. Take me and packing my suitcase. If I was honest with myself, I could probably sit down with a piece of paper and figure out 90 percent of the things I need to travel with every time. That might take me an hour of focused attention. But I don't want to invest that hour. So I take 20 minutes packing each time multiplied by those 300 flights in the last two years, for a total of 6,000 wasted minutes.

But if I was intentional, I'd have the mental capacity to figure out the patterns for success and eliminate as much wasted motion as possible. It wouldn't take me 20 minutes to pack, it'd take me 5 minutes with my trusted list. I would have saved 15 minutes, 300 different times. That's 4,500 minutes, or 75 hours, almost two solid workweeks. Should I have traded 60 minutes at the beginning for 4,500 minutes overall? I should have.

If I take the time up front, I can sharpen my packing skill to such a precise edge that I no longer have to think about it. Do you think that the Brazilian chef Alex Atala, whom we met in chapter 11, has to think when he cuts vegetables anymore? He's sharpened that skill so much it's a rote action. As Heidi Grant Halvorson, PhD, writes in her book *Succeed,* "We work best when as much of what we are doing can be delegated to the unconscious mind as possible."[2]

If we can make the activities that should be rote, deliberately rote, we free up a tremendous amount of brain space, time and energy to actually do new things for the first time. The more we can make something a routine, and stop giving it brainpower, the easier it is for us to apply that brainpower somewhere else in our life. I didn't invent that idea either.

On Christmas day, in the year 1876, author Gustave Flaubert wrote Gertrude Tennant and said, "Be regular and orderly in your life like a bourgeois, so that you may be violent and original in your work."[3] I'm almost positive that "bourgeois" is French for "people who wear powdered wigs," but that's not the point. The point is that your willingness to discipline one part of your life creates freedom in another.

This is a technique leaders throughout history have taken up. Like a guy named Albert Einstein. According to *Forbes*, "It has been reported that the famous physicist bought several versions of the same gray suit because he didn't want to waste brainpower on choosing an outfit each morning."[4]

President Barack Obama explained the idea even further, in an article in *Vanity Fair* written by Michael Lewis: "You also need to remove from your life the day-to-day problems that absorb most people for meaningful parts of their day. 'You'll see I wear only gray or blue suits,' [Obama] said. 'I'm trying to pare down decisions. I don't want to make decisions about what I'm eating or wearing. Because I have too many other decisions to make.'"[5]

If you think that won't work, I'd like to introduce you to the "speaking jeans" I own. For the last eighteen months, I've worn one pair of pants at every event I've spoken at. (The ones where jeans were acceptable onstage.) That's one less thing for me to think about when I pack.

■ Your Career Is Not Shampoo

The goal of repeating something the best way, in the right way, is so that you can do it without thinking. The more you can turn an important skill into a repeatable habit, the more you can trust the power of autopilot.

When I commuted to the Home Depot corporate offices in Atlanta, I didn't try a different route home every night. That would have been a stupid use of brainpower. Instead, I figured out one perfect route and then drove that one mindlessly. ("Perfect" is a relative term, given the soul-crushing nature of Atlanta traffic.)

Knowing how to get home gave me much-needed mental space for other thoughts and ideas. But what if the skill you want to work on isn't repeatable? Or even worse, what if repeating it over and over again, refusing to change it, makes it go dull?

That was what happened with me and blogging. I figured out how to write blogs in 2008 and then tried to put that on autopilot. Big mistake.

The rest of the blogging world moved on in fast cars and I found myself right back on the side of the road brushing my horse. These kids today with their opt-in e-mail addresses and Pinterest accounts! I got stuck doing the old way because it was the only way I knew. I refused to use photos. I wrote one-thousand-word-long diatribe-length posts despite all the evidence that readers wanted shorter pieces. Worst of all, I wouldn't admit that video had grown into an important component of blogging.

The answer of course isn't to throw out the baby with the bath water and just constantly change all the time, abandoning old skills that matter in the pursuit of new skills. Instead, you have to step into the tension of skills. You must repeat what needs to be repeated and also innovate what needs to be innovated.

Some skills can't and shouldn't be put on autopilot. Instead they should be put on fighter pilot. Every day should bring a new mission: something bigger, more challenging and more difficult. You learned from a previous win, not so you could try that exact same thing again. I am awesome at playing basketball against six-year-olds. I swear I block so many of their shots. But I'm not six anymore. If I don't play more difficult competition, and try harder opportunities, my skills go soft.

They rust and the industry I'm in passes me by.

Don't get lapped by the next generation. Don't get a horse. Cars are here to stay. Social media has a spot for you. The world is moving quickly, but so can we. Put some skills on autopilot and some skills on fighter pilot. If you're ever confused about which is which, talk to someone in your industry who has ten more years of experience than you and someone who has ten years less experience than you.

The more experienced person will be able to tell you which skills are best suited for autopilot. They'll have insight into which skills haven't changed over time and are best learned once and then repeated. If you're a dental hygienist, for instance, people skills will always matter. You can learn how to engage and encourage people whose teeth you clean during your first year on the job. People will always want to be treated with respect and kindness.

The less experienced person you talk to, who will often be younger than you, can help you learn about new innovations in the industry. Continuing our dental example, a new hygienist who learned new tools like online booking and Skype consultations can help you become aware of new skills you might need.

To have the best Career Savings Account possible you must continually learn new skills and hone old ones.

Remember

- When you refuse to practice a skill today, it makes it harder to practice it tomorrow. Weeds of fear grow stronger the longer we wait to hustle. Get in the garden today!

▪ First times should be the worst times when it comes to learning a new skill. Learn it well once, put it on autopilot and then apply the brainpower you save to something more important.

▪ To stay sharp, hone current skills through repetition and grow new ones through innovation.

15

Grab the Right Kind of Hammer for Your Career Ceiling

The father of every good work is discontent, and its
mother is diligence.
—LAJOS KASSAK

You will need skills most when you find yourself stuck.

When you experience a Career Ceiling, you are wedged firmly into the upper-left portion of our Do Over chart. You are voluntarily going to a negative work experience. Perhaps the ceiling is real. You have climbed to the end of a ladder at the job you have and now face a decision. Perhaps the ceiling is one that you set for yourself, but life just got busy. You promised yourself you wouldn't still be at this job by next spring. That was three springs ago and a temporary job has become permanent. Perhaps your ceiling is made of fear. Matt Wilson's is.

Matt is an X-ray technician. His boss is horrible, just a miserable human being. The practice he works for is poorly run and everyone hates their job. But no one leaves. I asked Matt about that one day. I wanted to know why he didn't look for another job. He said, "Jon, there are a lot of unemployed X-ray technicians right now."

Technically, he was right. There are. I'm sure right now there are a lot of technicians like Matt who do not have jobs. This isn't the easiest economy for some professions. But let's be honest about that logic. Should you ever stay at a bad job just because other people in your field don't have a job? What are you really saying? That until everyone in your field is employed you can't apply somewhere else? You can't have another job until everyone else does? That doesn't make any sense.

There will always be unemployed X-ray technicians, but Matt is deciding to use that excuse as part of his prison. That is what it means to be stuck, building your own cage and then beating against the bars in frustration as if you weren't the architect.

We need skills for this very moment because when we are stuck we really only have two options. We can choose it or we can change it.

When we choose it, we unknowingly decide that this is our lot in life. It is what it is. We build elaborate internal campaigns justifying where we are. We trick ourselves into thinking it's someone else's fault or that maybe it's not so bad. It's not a horrible job, it's a good-enough job. If we stay there long enough, we eventually forget that we are even allowed to change.

It's like the scene in *The Shawshank Redemption* when Morgan Freeman's character is finally released from prison after spending most of his life there. One of the saddest scenes in a movie full of sad scenes is when he asks the manager of a grocery store he works at if he can go to the bathroom. Irritated by the request, his boss calls him over and tells him he doesn't need to ask every time he wants to go to the bathroom. He says, "Just go. Understand?"[1]

Though many of us haven't been to prison, we've all had friends we wanted to tell "Just go!" The mistakes they were making, the places they were staying stuck, the bad job that would never get better or their bad attitude that was making every job bad, we could see it all and eventually our compassion turned to frustration because it was so obvious. They were choosing to stay stuck.

And we all do this sometimes. I got stuck for six months after my last Do Over. I had made a big decision to quit my job, but suddenly didn't know what to do next. I didn't know which direction to head. I wanted a thirty-year plan that perfectly aimed me in the 100 percent guaranteed correct direction. Despite often telling other people "You don't need to figure your whole life out before you take some steps," I was refusing to move in my own life. I put on twenty-five pounds, mostly queso weight, listened to mopey music and settled into stuck. Eventually, though, I decided to explore the second option we have when we bump into Career Ceilings. I decided to change it.

I can't predict the future, but I can change the present.

I can't tell you if in ten years I will have written five more books. But I can tell you that this year I will write one.

I can't tell you if in ten years my blog will have five million readers, but I can write a new post today.

I can't tell you if in ten years I'll be doing a TED talk but I can write a speech for a local event next week.

Once I decided that I would not choose to stay stuck, I was able to start seeing skills I could work on. I think most of our skills are developed in life when we run into ceilings. Skills are a hammer. They help us break through ceilings. Prior to that moment, we never had a reason to develop them until we got stuck.

Bumping into a ceiling isn't failure, it is training. The ceilings are designed to test your mettle and see if you really have what it takes to finish anything and break through to the next level.

The ceiling is actually the jungle that keeps most people away from the hidden treasure. And if you're ready to work on the skills category of your Career Savings Account, this is a tremendous gift. Author Seth Godin calls it the "Dip." He says, "The Dip is the set of artificial screens set up to keep people like you out. If you took organic chemistry in college, you've experienced the Dip. Academia doesn't want too many unmotivated people to attempt medical school, so they set up a screen. Organic chemistry is the killer class, the screen that separates the doctors from the psychologists. If you can't handle organic chemistry, well, then you can't go to med school."[2]

Godin's right: The ceilings are designed to filter out the lazy and uncommitted.

Be careful when you run into a ceiling. Bitterness can grow quickly in the quiet corners of one. Once, when I encountered a ceiling at a job, instead of working on my skills, I worked on my sulk. Instead of recognizing it for what it was and deciding which skills I would use to break through it, I got angry. I became a jerk to people around me, blaming them for the ceiling versus actually doing something about it. I should have focused on my skills and gone to another job eventually. Instead of hustling on skills, I hustled on bitterness. It was like I turned on rocket boosters in a room with a roof, burning all the bridges around me.

Breaking through a ceiling doesn't mean you have to quit your job. If you want to use your CSA to have an amazing career at a big company, go for it. You can do important, world-changing work at big companies too, not just at small start-ups.

If you're not stuck right now, awesome. Keep learning new skills, keep sharpening old ones and hopefully you'll never get stuck. If you are, though, if you find yourself pressed against some ceiling, don't just bang your head. Don't waste time bemoaning the situation. Don't ignore how stiff your neck feels for a second longer.

Grab the skill note cards you made and think of each one like a hammer. Ask yourself, "Why have I hit a Career Ceiling and which of the skills that I currently possess will help me break through it?"

If, as you look at the cards, you discover you don't currently have the right hammer, ask, "What new skill do I need to learn?"

If both of these questions feel difficult to wade through, go back to one of the friends you identified in the relationship exercises and ask for help. It's amazing what other people can identify about our Career Ceilings and skills.

I thought I had run into an unbreakable ceiling when I worked at Bose, the stereo company in Framingham, Massachusetts. Had I possessed the maturity to ask a friend, though, I think he would have seen then what I see now. Bose was an amazing company to work for. I hadn't hit a ceiling; that company was full of new opportunities to explore. In my frustration I stayed stuck because I didn't grab the right hammer.

I hope you will.

Every skill can be a hammer.

Start banging.

Career Ceilings were meant to be broken.

Investment 3
CHARACTER

Who you are.

Voluntary

Career
Jump
(Character Investment)

Positive

Investment 3: Character

A talent is formed in stillness, a character in the world's torrent.

—JOHANN WOLFGANG VON GOETHE

If relationships are who you know and skills are what you do, character is who you are.

Since religion, science and philosophy have been trying to get to the bottom of that question for thousands of years I thought I would go ahead and figure it out for us all in this next section. You're welcome.

Or, instead, I could tell you how character impacts your work and why you need it in your Career Savings Account.

Character is the mortar between all the other parts of the Career Savings Account. It's what holds the other things together. Relationships get you the first gig. Skills get you the second. Character is the reason that people will still want to give you another chance if the first opportunity fails. It's also the reason that, when it all comes together, you don't come apart, drunk on ego or success.

If you have amazing skills, tremendous hustle, lots of relationships but no character you end up like any number of athletes who have fallen from grace. Or politicians. Or rock stars. Or watch TMZ for nineteen seconds and pick out your own favorite example.

Without character, you also won't have strong relationships. You can have quantity but not quality, for strong character is a prerequisite to strong relationships. No two items in the Career Savings Account are linked together as strongly as character and relationships. If you have no character, people won't want to be around you. They might work with you for now because they need some skill you offer, but the minute they can find a different or cheaper place to get it, they will abandon you.

Why is it important that you have personal character when it comes to your career? Because everything is personal in work. We culturally tend to believe that when it comes to our careers, "it's not personal, it's just business."

That logic works well if you're having a conversation with your computer explaining why you're upgrading to a new one, but if you're actually interacting with another human, it falls apart. Everything we do has personal consequences. The more we believe it's just business, the easier it gets to do some fairly dastardly things to each other.

Character is a competitive advantage. When people say, "All those candidates have the skills we need but there's just something about that last one I can't put my finger on," they're talking about character. Character, though hard to measure, is often impossible to ignore.

Character is also what you need the most when you make a positive, voluntary career transition, or what we're calling a "Career Jump." You need it the most then because it will be tested the most when you "just go for it" or "chase a dream." When you make a jump, you will be tempted to cut corners, to quit when the going gets tough and lose your patience when the results you expected don't immediately happen. In those moments, when friends think you're crazy for trying, your skills don't feel like enough and your hustle is exhausted, it is your character that will push you forward.

Perhaps best of all, character has the messiest borders and will spread to other areas of your life when you focus on it in your career. The character lessons we're about to master will positively impact your family and friends. Your doorway to them might be through a Career Do Over, your practice space a job, but character traits are contagious. Character goes viral.

Whether you're stuck at a job, out of work, chasing a dream or facing a second career, there will never be a job situation that cannot benefit from character. (Unless you're in the Mob. Matter of fact, I should have said that earlier in the book. I hope you've been reading this whole time with the filter "unless you're in the Mob.")

The goal of this section is to help you become the type of person people want to work with. We're going to accomplish this by planting an orchard and being generous, empathetic and present.

▪ Wait, Wait, Wait. Don't Bad Guys Win Sometimes?

They do. Not even sometimes, a lot of times.

It's easy to think of people in the news or people you actually know who are winning despite their lack of character. You've had a boss who kept getting promoted despite not having any character. Or maybe in some cases you even worked for someone who got promoted because they lacked character and were willing to do some things to win that no one else would do.

I'm not going to argue that strong character is the only way to win. It's not.

It's just the best way. The one that leaves you with relationships intact. The one that protects your name and reputation. The one that makes it easier to sleep at night. Sure, bad guys win, but they're often pretty miserable during the process. And the win is always temporary. How do I know? I've seen their funerals.

Want to see who had character and who didn't? Attend a funeral. The proof is usually seen in who attends and what is said. Will the rows be empty or full? Will people who barely knew you mutter the equivalent of stock photography sentences about your life, or will dear friends laugh and cry together, celebrating a life lived fully? Your character and what you did with it will determine that more than anything else in your life.

16

Plant an Orchard

The future is purchased by the present.
—DR. SAMUEL JOHNSON

Character is the worst. I know I just said it was the best and got all public-service-announcement there about funerals, but it's also the worst. The reason it bothers me so much is that it takes forever.

The other three investments in the Career Savings Account have more immediate results. You can call a friend you haven't talked to in a while and work on your relationship today. You can sign up for a class to improve a skill or get up early and hustle. But character? That's a slow burn. Character is leg day at the gym when deep down you know you want to do chest and biceps. Nobody likes leg day. It's not even like growing a garden, which I am told is a very slow process. Character takes even longer than that.

It's also an incredibly fuzzy topic. There are a thousand ways to define it, discuss it and debate it. For our purposes I'm going to use a simple metaphor to describe it.

Character is an orchard.

What do orchards have? Trees, weeds and farmers.

You're the farmer. For the ninety-two bajillion people who have already worked fictional farms online with popular apps, you should feel right at home. And people told you growing fake digital corn would never pay off! For the rest of you, don't worry, there will be no actual overalls or pitchforks involved in this chapter.

The trees are your character traits. They need to be planted, watered, tended and deliberately grown.

The weeds are all the things that threaten to destroy your orchard. The challenge is that they tend to grow a lot faster than the trees. They can pop up seemingly overnight.

Full trees? Mature trees? That takes a while. You won't see as many results as you want to at first.

You don't get any apples the first year you have an orchard. There aren't bushels of delicious fruit rolling down your hills. The second year you don't get many either. It can take five years for you to get enough for a pie, that you'll probably drop on the floor because you're so excited you had enough apples to make a pie.

That's why there's an old saying: "The best time to plant a tree was twenty years ago. The second best time is now."

We don't have access to twenty years ago, but we do have right now, which is why we're going to start with a single tree.

■ The First Tree

What's one character trait, related to your career, that you'd like to grow stronger?

Don't pick three or five. Like everything else we've done in this book, pick one. And don't pick your strongest character trait. If you're known the world over for your patience, that's great. You've got a strong, mature sequoia full of watermelon planted in your orchard. I'm nearing the end of my tree knowledge.

I don't want you to add one extra branch to a tree that is already strong, I want you to plant a seedling. Something small, that you'd like to grow. Remember, we're adding a new tree to our orchard because when we make a Career Jump it will be our character that is tested the most. We want the biggest orchard possible for moments like that.

Sometimes asking ourselves that question is enough, other times we have to dig for the answer.

If you don't want to explore this question alone, ask a friend out to coffee. If you've done everything suggested in the book thus far, this will constitute the fiftieth coffee with that friend. Or you can just have one massive "Help me figure out my career" super coffee summit with an advocate where you discuss everything. Really up to you.

Be brave and ask them what career-centered character trait could use a little work in your life. Please know that if my friend told me anything other than "You're perfect the way you are," my initial reaction would be to storm away from the table in a huff, possibly punching someone eating a scone as I kicked the exit door open. I'm immature, though, and a scone killed my uncle so you'll probably react better to the honest feedback from a friend.

Perhaps perfectionism is a character flaw you need to work on. Coworkers wince when they get put on a project with you because they know you're going to grind every last ounce of joy out of the work in your pursuit of perfection.

Maybe trust is something to work on at your job. Though it might feel temporarily good to gossip about someone else, it erodes the confidence people have in us. If you want to increase trust, you'll have to decrease the negative things you say about other people.

Focus on taking responsibility for your mistakes if that's a character trait you want to whip into shape. It's easier to blame other people for our shortfalls but we only get to strengthen the things we take responsibility for.

If you can't find one work-related character trait you want to grow stronger because you're already perfect, then just write down "honesty." Because you are clearly a liar.

■ Take a Look at the Whole Orchard

If you're not ready to look at a specific character trait, take a wider, broader view of your orchard. If you flew over it with a helicopter, what pattern about your career would emerge?

I used to think my pattern was simple:

1. Get hired at new job.

2. Enjoy it for six months.

3. Get bored.

4. Get bitter.

5. Leave.

6. Repeat at a new job.

While I was writing this book, though, I started to notice that wasn't the whole pattern. The whole pattern was this:

1. Get hired at new job.

2. Enjoy it for six months.

3. Get bored.

4. Get bitter.

5. Almost get fired.

6. Plot an epic comeback.

7. Make the company fall back in love with me through hard work.

8. Leave.

9. Repeat at a new job.

Sometimes if I overplayed my hand in step 5, I never got to launch steps 6–7 and instead got fired. Sitting down and realizing I did that revealed that my core character issue wasn't boredom or bitterness. It was chaos. At every job, I created chaos of some sort. If things were going along well, I would throw a grenade into them, often sabotaging myself.

This pattern has already started manifesting itself in my current Do Over. When I left my last job, my youngest daughter said, "Dad doesn't have a job anymore." My oldest daughter immediately replied, "Yeah he does, it's to actually be around now." That was a tiny little fist into my stomach, but she was speaking the truth. Part of the reason I left my last job was because I was on the road a lot. When my daughter said that to me, I promised myself I'd do a better job being home.

Fast-forward a year and I spent more time on the road working for myself than I did at my last company. Why? Because I like the chaos of travel. I like to fill my schedule so full that it's chaotic. Speaking in Myrtle Beach, South Carolina, Omaha, Nebraska, and Lancaster, Pennsylvania, in ninety-six hours is chaos. It wasn't my last job or my last boss that kept me on the road, it was my addiction to chaos, and I've already found a new way to feed it as I work for myself.

Recognizing that, grasping that gift of awareness we've talked about a lot in this book, allows me to start working on it. I'll always travel as part of my job and I love getting to speak to clients, but when I do it out of chaos, my character falls apart.

If you've had more than one job, you've developed a pattern too. In the same ways we looked for consistency in the skills we possess, you need to look for consistency in the character you possess.

We all have patterns. They'll either conform us in good ways, allowing character traits to take deep roots for great results, or control us in bad ways, allowing weeds to take over the entire orchard.

Pull back on your career and take a look at what your pattern might be trying to tell you. To do that, try these four steps in a notebook since I promised no more note cards:

1. Write down the jobs you've had.

Include any part-time and full-time positions.

2. Give a brief description of your job performance.

Were you promoted? Did you get good annual reviews? Did you get reprimanded?

3. List the way you left each job.

Were you fired? Did you move out of state? Did you get a better offer from another company?

4. Describe the strength of the relationships you left behind.

Would it be awkward to run into former coworkers at a coffee shop? Did they ask you to do freelance work for them even though you no longer worked there? Did your boss write you a great referral?

The answers don't have to be long. Mine would look like this:

1. I worked for Bose.

2. I was promoted and given a great position, but reprimanded for my bad attitude and lack of effort at times. (As mentioned, I incorrectly thought it was a Career Ceiling.)

3. I left Massachusetts and moved to Georgia, which forced me to leave the company.

4. The relationships remained intact. They offered to let me work from Atlanta full time if I wanted to and then gave me freelance work to do after I had left.

Do that for each job you've had and then look for what those experiences have in common. If the answer to question 3 is always "I got a better job offer from another company," that's great. Your work performance and ability to build relationships outside of your company must be trees you've planted firmly in your orchard. If the answer to question 4 for every job you've ever had is "They're all dead to me," it might be time to pull some weeds.

■ Pull These Weeds as Fast as You Can

The rest of the character section is going to be a discussion on the three trees that will have the greatest impact on your Career Savings Account.

Before we talk about planting and growing them, we need to make sure we've pulled a few weeds. Character is tricky like that. You often don't notice it until it's gone. If I asked you to name five people you've worked with who had strong character, it would take you a lot longer than if I asked you to name five people who have no character. We tend to remember the knives in our back easier than the pats on our back.

Those people, the ones you couldn't stand working with, all had one thing in common—they lacked character. Their orchards were choked by these workplace weeds:

1. Narcissism

I completely get the irony of someone who has a picture of his headshot inside the cover of a book telling you about narcissism but life is ironic. When it comes to character the weed of narcissism is the belief that you're the only one who matters at the company. The company is there for your benefit and the phrase "Take one for the team" is your kryptonite. This is the one I struggle with the most, possibly compounded by the fact that car services pick me up with a little sign in baggage claim when I fly to an event. Recently while heading to the limo, I pressed the #2 button in the elevator for the floor we were parked on. The driver said, "Sir, please do not do that. You are a guest." He's right! These are typing fingers, not elevator-pushing fingers. I can't be using my hands that way! I'm Jon Acuff! These are callus-free writer hands. I can't sully them like normal people! (I can't pull the narcissism weeds in my orchard; I usually have to use a flamethrower because there are so many.)

2. Dishonesty

This weed comes in a tremendous amount of varieties. Dishonesty at work can mean simple lying. Someone said they did something that they did not do. They covered a small mistake with a slightly bigger lie. Dishonesty can also take the form of gossip. When you talk bad about someone else behind their back, you're lying to their face if you're friendly when you see them. Dishonesty can also mean overpromising and underdelivering. I might pretend I wrestle with this because I don't want to disappoint people, but when I promise them a timeline I know I will never hit, I'm lying. In my defense this might be caused by the exhausting amount of elevator buttons I've been pressing all by myself lately.

3. Pessimism

Oh, you little black cloud, you. Eeyore of Winnie the Pooh fame would bump into you and think, "I get why I'm sad. Someone stuck my tail on with a nail gun, but what's that guy's problem?" People who only have the ability to see the negative and then the gift to spread the negative aren't fun to work with. This can morph into paranoia as well, as a coworker starts to operate from an "I'm under attack" perspective. Sometimes when I get voicemails my first thought is, "That's someone calling to tell me I've screwed up something." I can't explain why I live from a "called to the principal's office" point of view, but I do. If I'm not careful, that pessimism weed grows until I can no longer brainstorm and dream, two activities that require the optimism of creativity.

4. Apathy

People who don't care about their jobs don't have to worry about having jobs for very long. This is one of the easiest weeds to see in someone else. It's the surly service on the phone call, the lazy attention to details and the general "whatever" that floods a coworker's every action. Most destructive of all is that apathy cripples your ability to launch a Career Jump. No one who is apathetic has the energy or heart to try a positive, voluntary career transition. That entire quadrant is off the table when weeds like this have grown in your orchard.

The frustrating thing about those four things is that they all apply to me. The weeds we can't stand in others are often the weeds we've been ignoring in our own orchards.

Before you start to plant generosity, empathy and presence, make sure you've got a handle on your weeds.

If you have a hard time finding any, spend sixty seconds thinking about someone who you really didn't like working with. What weeds were present in their orchard? Once you've got a sense of that, flip the question and ask, "Are those my weeds, too?"

I once worked with someone who was a horrific pessimist. Every minute I spent with him felt like being with a vampire that fed on joy. I was so glad I was not like him. Right up until the moment I made my wife cry while we were brainstorming the marketing of this book. I was shooting down every one of her ideas with elaborate reasons it wouldn't work. When she suggested I tweet people songs I like as part of a thirty-days-of-encouragement idea, I said, "I don't own the copyrights though. I couldn't e-mail a link to a song without getting permission from Sting first." I'm not sure if you were aware of that rule. In order to tweet out a link to a song you like on YouTube you have to call Sting personally. Every little breath I guess.

Turns out I have some weeds. If you do too, start pulling. We've got some tree planting to do!

Remember

■ Relationships get you the first gig and skills get you the second. Character helps ensure that if you fail you'll get another shot and if you succeed you won't get drunk on ego.

■ Character takes time. Start with a single trait (or tree) you'd like to plant today. Orchards aren't grown overnight.

■ Look beyond one tree and see if your career has a pattern. From individual trees to flyover moments of the whole orchard, we need to know what's really going on in our career.

■ Workplace weeds ruin many orchards. Stay on the alert for narcissism, dishonesty, pessimism and apathy.

17

Generosity Is a Game Changer

*Service is renewing. When we serve, our work itself will
sustain us.*
—RACHEL NAOMI REMEN

On Good Friday, an important day for pastors like him, my dad rearranged his entire day for a five-hour round-trip visit to hear me speak for thirty minutes at a college. He then waited another hour while I interacted with students after the speech.

We then returned to Chapel Hill, North Carolina, so my dad could lead the Good Friday service. Later that day, he mentioned that he was going to do a private Easter service for a seventeen-year-old in the hospital.

The young man in question had fallen into a coma, struck down by something doctors could not identify. He had been removed from life support, only to regain consciousness. In the weeks that followed he had a heart transplant and was slowly recovering. My dad had been asked by the family to bring Easter to the ICU for that boy.

"You want to go with me tomorrow, Jon?" he asked. "I think it might be a pretty special moment." Without thinking for a second I said, "Probably not. But let me think about it."

I essentially said no.

Then my wife reminded me, "Well your dad did just drive five hours to see you speak."

Ugh.

Generosity, or really even common courtesy, is often not my first response in situations. I can't start a chapter about generosity as if that's a tall tree I've got in my orchard. It's not.

So I write this section not as someone who has mastered it and returned with wisdom from upon high to share with the greedy masses. I write this as someone prone to greed, stuck in the middle of the mud, trying to claw his way back to generosity. And if that's even a little bit like you, I hope this section helps us both because if we're going to have meaningful careers, we'll need generosity.

Perhaps we should start, though, by looking at why it matters to your career.

■ Generosity Creates Loyalty

When I did my Career Jump in 2013 and left the Dave Ramsey team, a good friend reached out immediately. Within days he had offered me a plan for the future that would ensure the Acuffs did not have to dance for our money on the streets of Nashville in 2014. It was incredibly generous and could not have been better timed.

A year later he offered me a new contract for 2015. I asked my father-in-law what I should charge this friend for the next year. The amount of work had increased between 2014 and 2015. I thought I should raise my rate.

My father-in-law, who helps run a billion-dollar company, surprised me with his answer.

"Tell him whatever he thinks is fair works for you."

He didn't say this as a form of negotiation or manipulation. He said this because the friend had been generous to me. At a time of great need, he had met me with great generosity. In return for that, the least I could do is be loyal for another year. And more than that, because of his initial generosity I could trust that he was not waiting to spring a trap of greed.

Generosity breeds loyalty. You will go to bat for people who have shown you generosity. Your employees will work harder. Your clients will return more often. When you are down, people will look for opportunities to pick you up. When you do something risky, like a Career Jump, people will make excuses to find ways to support you.

The number of people who show up to help you will be proportional to the amount of character you've invested in your relationships before your Career Jump.

More character leads to more friends, which leads to more help when you make a Career Jump.

The tricky thing is that *during* a Career Jump it's tempting to get greedy. Launching a positive, voluntary career transition is scary.

Fear will tell you to tighten your belt. Fear will say this is no time for generosity. This is the season to hold back your resources and time from others now that you've done something risky. You might have initially jumped with an open hand, but the jolt of reality as your feet hit the ground after a big jump encourages you to clinch your fists tightly.

A belief in scarcity comes into play as we fear there's not enough opportunity to go around for all of us. Best grab what we can!

We might find it easy to judge looters after storms that steal TVs but lots of us throw metaphorical trash cans through windows when we feel like opportunities are running out. That's how I felt when this book was released.

I didn't want to be generous and help people promote their books, even friends of mine. Granted, I hope to sell 100,000 copies of this book in the first year and there are over 200 million people who can read in the United States. But what if some other author gets those exact 100,000 people I was trying to sell my book to?

By the time I get to your front door you'll say, "Oh, I wish I had known you had a new book, Jon. I already bought a book from a different guy and that was the last one I plan on buying from now until I die." I'll shuffle away from your front stoop, confused at why I'm selling books door to door, but ultimately realizing it doesn't matter. It's too late. I'll never sell another book, having launched a Career Jump and written a book I've learned there just aren't enough book readers to go around. I'll have to move my family to a van down by the river. We'll end up eating my two-sided leather belt from T.J. Maxx for sustenance. (Brown side for dinner, black side for special occasions like Thanksgiving.)

Will that happen? Probably not, but you'd be surprised at the vivid, crazy pictures fear uses to make you greedy when you make a jump. Fight it by being generous.

Before you make a Career Jump give generously of your time, talent and resources without keeping score. If you keep a record of who you've been generous to with the expectation that they'll return the favor, you'll build transactions not relationships.

During a Career Jump give generously as a way to beat back the weed of greed. (That rhyme was unavoidable.) Greed will end up costing you a lot more than you think.

▪ Generosity Is Always Cheaper Than Greed

There are few things in the world that will change someone's opinion of you as quickly as your generosity.

Your willingness to be openhanded with people in the course of your career will pay you dividends for years and years and years. The problem is that we often think when it comes to our jobs, other people have to lose in order for us to win.

Roy H. Williams, the marketing expert we discussed earlier,

writes about this phenomenon in his book *The Wizard of Ads*. During the course of a business negotiation someone pushed hard for their side until the client was about to walk away from the deal. The bully in the meeting said, "I just wanted to be sure I wasn't leaving anything on the table."[1]

Williams's response to that is, "I believe there are times to leave something on the table. When you hope to do business with someone again, leave a little on the table. When you want a person to speak well of you, leave a little on the table. When you want to make someone your ally and your friend, be sure every deal is good for him, too, and change the deal when it's not."[2]

That's the key to generosity. It might not seem like a great short-term play, but I promise it's an amazing long-term play. The challenge is that greed is not something you can turn on and off. It's a toxin that ends up flavoring all of your interactions, regardless of what's really at stake.

Bill "not his real name because I didn't want to burn a bridge for him" Smith worked for a multimillion-dollar company. His boss was doing very well for himself. He had a private plane, a fleet of companies he owned and probably his own falcon. I don't know about the falcon but that's probably one of the first things I would

buy if I became absurdly rich. I guess you prefer to catch rabbits by hand, but to each his own.

One day, in the fifth year Bill had worked for this small thirty-person company, he asked his boss about tickets to a big college football game. His alma mater was playing in the game and he knew the boss had a few tickets he wasn't planning to use. Bill wanted to buy them from his boss and asked him how much they were.

Bill's boss e-mailed him back and said, "Sure, I have tickets! The face value on them is $200, but I've seen them going online for $400. Why don't you make me an offer?"

Greed.

Bill's boss is a millionaire. In that moment he was hoping to make $200–$500 by selling his tickets to his employee. You can't gas a private plane for that.

Bill, on the other hand, made around $45,000 a year. He'd given that company five years of his life. He was one of their best employees. I say "was" because he quit a few months later. He hated working for someone so greedy and the tickets were the final straw that broke the camel's back.

For the possibility of earning an extra $200 per ticket, Bill's boss lost a good employee. An employee who, by the way, was managing hundreds of thousands of dollars every year for the company. That's an expensive gamble, especially when you consider Bill wasn't asking his boss to give him the tickets for free. The boss would have broken even, not losing a dollar and not losing an employee. In the long run, greed always costs you more than generosity.

As you work on your Career Do Over, you will face intersections like the one Bill's boss did. Every career has moments like that. Bill's boss is not evil; if anything, he might have just been busy. He didn't stop to ask a powerful question about his decision, which was "What is really at stake right now?"

If he had, he never would have traded a valuable employee for the chance at $500.

At your current job, at your next job too, stop and ask that question. What is really at stake right now? Is a relationship worth more than $500? Is helping a new coworker get acclimated worth four hours of your month? Or, in other words, 2.5 percent? Pausing to run the real math can clarify what decision you're really facing. Adding generosity to your orchard can add tremendous value to your Career Savings Account.

■ Won't People Take Advantage of You?

Yes. Some will.

The world is full of greedy people. There are two fewer now that you and I have agreed to be generous, but you will run into people who misinterpret your act of generosity as an invitation to walk all over you. When you run into people like that, do the following:

1. Make sure you don't have an itchy trigger finger.

Is the coworker in question genuinely trying to take advantage of you or do you define "greed" as "anyone who bothers me at work while I am very clearly wearing huge headphones?" Maybe the guy who needs an occasional favor isn't greedy, you're just oversensitive. Don't forget to take off your foe goggles.

2. Draw some boundaries.

Being generous doesn't mean being foolish. It's perfectly fine to establish some boundaries around your life to help you create healthy relationships. Don't assume generosity is a weakness. It's actually a strength. Sometimes refusing to help someone and allowing them to learn their own lesson is the kindest thing you can do. In the ninth grade, while every other student was doing massive reports on John Quincy Adams and Abraham Lincoln for our school's "History Day" event, I chose to cover "The History of Rap." This was a terrible idea. You'd be surprised how underwhelmed the judges were at my knowledge of Kool Moe Dee and Big Daddy Kane. My parents could have stepped in and done the project for me, but they didn't. Their refusal to help wasn't a bad thing. I learned a cornucopia of lessons from that experience. (For more on the topic of boundaries read the book *Boundaries* by Henry Cloud and John Townsend.)

3. Avoid them.

Remember what we give foes? Distance! If your habit of generosity is continually abused by someone, avoid that person. If that person is your boss, reread page 50.

Need further proof that generosity is important to your career? Read that list again and imagine you're the culprit being discussed right now who is greedy. Eventually, coworkers and the opportunities they have will avoid you if you're not generous.

■ Make Your Definition of Generosity Bigger

Most of the time, when we think about being generous we think about giving people money. That might not always work in the context of a Career Do Over. I imagine you walking through the halls of your job shaking hands with people and slipping them cash. Greasing some palms! Standing at the front door of a place you want to work handing every employee a dollar as they start the day. Raining down cash from the balcony of an open-air cafeteria. Even though those all sound delightful, I do not recommend them.

Though generosity can be monetary—in the form of salary, raises and prices—your current job might not offer you the opportunity to be generous with any of those things. Fortunately, there are two things you have that you can be generous with: your time and your skills.

This approach has its own set of baggage associated with it, though. When we think about giving our time, we assume it has to suck. Let's go ahead and be honest about that. When we think about serving we imagine doing something horrible for a few hours out of obligation.

But where does it say that being generous has to be miserable?

I'm a writer. Writing is what I do. It's what I'm best at. So then why, when I think about being generous, do I never think about using my writing? Why is my first thought, "I better find a circular saw and a family that needs me to build them a new set of stairs"? I'm horrible at construction. I don't know anything about wood-work. So when I define being generous as spending lots of time do-ing something I'm miserable at, of course I'll hate the idea of being generous with my time. And some poor family will probably get a poorly constructed set of steps that eventually murders them as they leave their house to go to the grocery store.

What if we were able to match up our skills and our hustle with our generosity? What if being generous meant more than just money or time but actually talent? Maybe helping people write their resumes is what I need to do while my brother-in-law, who works in construction, is the one who needs to build that staircase.

Will I still paint houses and clean up the neighborhood if that's what my community needs? Of course, otherwise you end up like Steve Buscemi's character in the *The Incredible Burt Wonderstone* movie, giving magic kits to people who needed food instead.

To apply this to a Career Do Over, get out your relationship and skill note cards. Spread them all out. Now pick one work-related re-lationship you're going to be generous to. Now pick one skill you're going to be generous with in that relationship.

Maybe Jeff the business analyst sends out long business requirement documents to the team for feedback before he sends them to your supervisor. No one gives him any feedback because they are long business requirement documents. What if this week, instead of just deleting his e-mail, you printed out the documents? Spend an hour reviewing them. Help Jeff by finding typos, raising questions and adding value where you can. Is that your direct role? Maybe not, but he'll see that as you helping him fix mistakes using your skills before the boss finds them.

You gave Jeff an hour of your time and your proofreading skill, but you did much more than that.

You threw a relational boomerang.

You built some loyalty with Jeff.

You strengthened your relationship with Jeff.

You opened the door to some new project opportunities with Jeff.

That's the big power of even the smallest act of generosity.

Remember

- Generosity creates loyalty, something you'll be glad you have during a Career Jump.

- The world is not running out of opportunities; ignore fear when it tells you to be greedy.

- Generosity is always cheaper than greed. Count the true cost of what's at stake when you make decisions.

- Give chronically greedy people the same thing you give foes— distance.

- Make your definition of generosity bigger by being generous with your skills and time, not just your money.

18

Empathy, No Longer Just for People Who Like to Cry with Friends

It is well to remember that the entire population of the universe, with one trifling exception, is composed of others.
—JOHN ANDREW HOLMES

At the core of all four transitions is the word "new." Whether you have a Career Bump, Ceiling, Opportunity or Jump, you will find yourself awash in new during a Do Over. You'll have to face new skills, new relationships, new jobs, new challenges and new clients. The best way to navigate this new storm is with one key character trait—empathy.

Though it may sound soft or like the name of Celine Dion's celebrity perfume, empathy plays an important role in your Career Savings Account.

To jump into this discussion, let's begin with a new definition of the word in question.

Empathy = Understanding someone else's needs and acting on them.

As you launch a Career Jump, the filter of empathy will help you acclimate to new situations if you accomplish both parts of the definition. Getting one-half right is easy, anyone can do that. You've experienced plenty of businesses that got half of the definition correct. The customer service representative, who constantly tells you, "We are so sorry and regret your inconvenience," but doesn't fix your problem is only addressing the "understanding someone's needs" part. The business that launches a major product without asking if customers really want it is living out the second half of the definition.

Half empathy is better than no empathy but it doesn't change your career and it certainly won't change the world.

Empathy need not be complicated. It can be pretty straightforward. Here's my secret to empathy: believe that everyone is the same.

That's it. I probably won't put that on a mug because it's so boring but it's true. The people you work with or work for are just like you. They have the same hopes and fears and dreams and frustrations that you do. They express them differently, but that doesn't mean they're really that different from you.

I learned this one morning talking on a radio show for truckers.

I know what you're thinking. "If there's anything Jon Acuff knows about, it's hauling a rig across state lines."

It's true, I've spent many years on the highways and byways living the life of a trucker. I've even been known to win a roadside arm-wrestling competition a time or two just by turning my hat backward.

Actually, I know very little about truck driving except that Penske shouldn't have rented me a twenty-four-foot beast of a truck just because I had a driver's license. I couldn't tell you a thing about the trucking industry. But, I know people. I know empathy.

I know how my wife feels when I have to travel for business. Is me speaking at a corporate business conference the same as driving a load of chickens to South Carolina? No. The executions are very different but the heart isn't. Even though I'm in an airport terminal, not a truck stop, the bottom line is the same for me and all those truckers: we're not home.

The day after I was on the radio show the producer thanked me for taking live calls from the truckers and helping them with their problems. She really felt like I understood the trucker life. I don't, but I understand the value of empathy. In the context of a career, empathy opens a thousand doors because it allows you to work with just about anyone.

Great salespeople have known this for years. The girl who can sell real estate could sell vacuums, websites and health insurance. Is she an expert in all of those fields? Maybe not, but she knows if you take the time to understand people and what they need, you don't have to be an expert in every product. You just have to be empathetic.

Dustin Brake was training to be a pharmacist. He got burned out on the profession after a few years and now loves his job of managing a jewelry store. Did he have an extensive background in rings, watches and necklaces when he launched his Career Jump? Nope. "I didn't know anything about jewelry," he told me, "but I did know people."

Want to expand your job opportunities, number of companies you can work at and teams you can work for? Realize that people are all the same. Embrace empathy and then combine it with generosity.

To do that you'll have to start with a story.

■ Take Time to Know Someone's Real Story

I had a hard time watching the show *Fear Factor*. They were constantly making people lie in coffins full of spiders, second on my list of fears after "stuck in a trash chute full of scorpions." The other reason I didn't watch that show was the host, Joe Rogan. He always struck me as a bit of a bully. He seemed angry for no reason and is often the most intense person at Ultimate Fighting Championship events, which is a difficult feat to accomplish.

When you put someone in a box or label them, though, it eliminates your ability to be empathetic.

That's what I did to Joe Rogan. I judged him. I put him in a bully box and moved on.

But that changed when I heard his story.

In an interview on Marc Maron's podcast, Joe Rogan shared how when he was four and five years old, he witnessed his father brutally beat his mother. Though Joe and his mother would later escape, watching that broke Joe in a way no kid should ever experience.[1]

In the conversation with Maron, Joe mused about how his fascination with karate and bodybuilding might be connected deeply to his desire to protect himself from physical violence. That maybe if he were strong and knew how to fight, nobody could hurt him.

Do you think I thought about Joe Rogan differently after I heard his story? Of course I did. And that's because stories wreck our ability to judge someone.

When you hear someone's story, they are no longer just an idea or an object, they become a human. They become a five-year-old who had terrifying things thrust on them or a twelve-year-old who never learned what it feels like to be safe or a single mom who is trying to balance three kids, a job and a million other responsibilities. Stories make 2-D people 3-D.

Author Stephen Covey experienced that on a subway one morning. There was a father whose kids were jumping around like maniacs. Few things drive other parents crazy as quickly as an inattentive parent and out-of-control kids. Finally, Covey pointed out that the kids were out of control. The dad, in a detached kind of way looked up and said, "Oh, you're right, I guess I should do something about it. We just came from the hospital where their mother died an hour ago. I don't know what to think, and I guess they don't know how to handle it either."[2] Knowing that changed Covey's ability to be empathetic and give that father what he needed in that moment: compassion.

Covey didn't know that family. I don't know Joe Rogan so it makes sense in both situations that it was difficult to know the real story at first. But what about with people we do know? People we work with. Why do we have a hard time with empathy? Because fear is an amazing storyteller.

The key to knowing someone's story is believing the real one, not the one fear tells us. Have you ever gotten an e-mail from your boss on Friday afternoon at 5 p.m.? It wasn't long and just said, "We need to talk about something on Monday. No big deal, but let's do it first thing. Have a good weekend!"

Good weekend? That's impossible now. You will spend the entire weekend scripting out the story of what that meeting is going to be in your head. You'll interview every mistake you've made in the last few months and come up with justifications for them. He's not your boss now, he's the prosecutor in a court case. You prepare an elaborate defense and show up defensive. (If you don't do that in your head, please tell me your secret for confidence and I'll tell you mine for anxiety-fueled night sweats.)

From the very get-go you've shaped how that conversation will go by having it first in your head. And you've put a lot of stories in your boss's mouth that probably aren't there. We do that with people all the time. From coworkers to family members.

My friend had a disagreement with his wife one morning. He spent the day adding words to that story she hadn't really said, amplifying the whole thing each time he replayed it in his imagination. When he got home, he apologized to her and said, "Sorry, I was lying in my head for you all day." He told himself a story that wasn't true.

Everybody has a story. When we don't take the time to know someone's story or worse, create our own version of it, we lose the chance to understand what they need, which is the first step to empathy.

■ Care About What the People You Care About Care About

It occurred to me that if you've never been empathetic before with coworkers, clients or vendors, it might be incredibly awkward to launch an "empathy campaign" this Monday. Just sidle up to a coworker, give them a small gift and say, "I'm here to talk about your needs, Tom. You ready to open up with your story, big guy?"

Turning on the empathy fire hose will probably get you strange looks in the break room. That's why character is an orchard, it's about making small changes over time.

If any of this chapter has made you uncomfortable, then great. It's working. Learning something new shouldn't be comfortable, but it is important if you're going to make a Career Jump.

If you feel like your particular job, company or career isn't suited for empathy, I'd like to introduce you to a chimney sweep I met. I'll refer to him as that dude from *Mary Poppins* because we're all thinking it. Or Joe because it's shorter.

I met Joe at a Chimney Sweep convention I was speaking at in

Branson, Missouri. (Remember when I said empathy opens you up to a wide variety of opportunities?) Joe realized that none of his regular customers looked at the direct mail campaigns he sent them. Try as he might, they would simply throw them away. Since chimney cleaning is the kind of annual service most people forget about, unless you have some sort of woodland beast trapped in there, Joe needed a way to remind his customers to get their chimneys cleaned.

So he thought to himself, "What in addition to clean chimneys do my customers care about?" He realized that a lot of his customers have dogs and they're very passionate about their pets.

So he tried something. Every time he was at someone's house who owned a dog, he would be really friendly to it. He'd pet it and tell the owner how cute it was. He'd ask if he could take a photo of it and if the owner said OK, he would. He'd then upload the photo to an app that turned images into postcards.

A few days later, he'd send the owner a postcard of the picture he took. In the corner was his name, phone number and website. He said to me:

"Pet owners never throw away photos of their pets. Do you

know what they do instead? They put the photo on the fridge. Do you know which of my other ads they put on the fridge? None."

There's definitely a healthy dose of hustle in what Joe did, something we'll learn about in the next section, but that all started with empathy. He thought about what people care about, realized they weren't waiting around for his next direct mail card and then brainstormed possible needs. His story is also a reminder that a Career Jump doesn't always mean quitting your job. In Joe's case, doing something positive and voluntary meant trying an innovative tweak to his business model.

Remember the coworker or client you were going to be generous with this week? What do they need? What's their motive? What's his or her photo of a dog? And when you find out what it is, what's a way you can do something about it?

Generosity and empathy are closely intertwined, they go hand in hand. The stronger you get in one, the stronger you'll get in the other. If you get good at them and this spills over into you remembering your next wedding anniversary, please let your spouse know they can send me a thank-you note.

■ Read Less Minds, Ask More Questions

Joe is not your average chimney sweep. He was gifted at understanding what people need, but what if you're not? What if you've actually tried before and it backfired? How do you figure out what a coworker, client or customer really needs?

Read less minds, ask more questions. (Right now, for instance, I know what grammar aficionados need is for that to say "Read fewer minds," but in this case being grammatically correct ruins the rhythm.)

Don't just try to guess what someone cares about. Take a shortcut and ask them. Bose, the electronics company known for headphones and home theater systems, did this when I was working on the launch of a new product for guitarists.

We knew that musicians in smoky bars didn't know us that well. They thought of Bose as clean, scientific and prone to bouts of classical music. Instead of trying to guess what guitar players wanted, we just asked them. We invited musicians from across the country to a special event called "Band Camp."

Instead of trying to read their minds, we asked them questions. In the process we learned about needs we never could have guessed. For instance, they asked us not to put our name on the outside of the bag the speakers came in. "Why?" we asked, puzzled at this request.

"When people at clubs see the name 'Bose' they realize I have expensive gear and steal it. I'm going to cover your name with tape or you can just leave it off the bag altogether." We never would have arrived at that conclusion if we had spent weeks brainstorming by ourselves.

Don't miss valuable chances to be empathetic in your career by just guessing what people need. Read less minds. Ask more questions.

▪ The Beginner's Version of Empathy

It's possible that chimney sweep was some sort of empathetic ninja, which I think is an oxymoron since whenever ninjas ask, "What does someone need?" the answer is, "To be stabbed with a sword." But let's say we're not ready for that level of empathy.

Here's a beginner's level of empathy I learned from Angie Smith.

Angie is a talented author and speaker who lives in our neighborhood. She has a huge platform and has generously shared it with me in the past, helping me sell books. She and her husband, Todd, have definitely been advocates in my Career Do Over.

Though that advocacy has certainly had some tactical implications and actions, the biggest one was when Angie did the simplest thing you can do to be empathetic. She showed up.

Jenny and I had reached a milestone in my Career Do Over. After six months, something had finally happened that we had been waiting for. Angie knew the date and what it meant to us. And she just showed up. At midnight. She was driving back from a speaking gig and her husband was out of town. Her nanny had put the kids to bed so no one was waiting up for her. Unannounced, she showed up at our doorstep while Jenny and I waited for the clock to hit midnight.

It was just an ordinary Thursday to everyone else but to Jenny and me, it was a big moment. And Angie showed up. She stayed until 2 A.M. laughing and talking and dreaming with us.

It wasn't complicated. It wasn't fancy. It might not even seem like much as you read those paragraphs, but if you've ever had someone show up, you know how much it matters. You know the difference it makes.

In the relationship section we talked a lot about asking people to help us, but who are we going to help? We need to be deliberate about showing up. Maybe empathy starts with you being more deliberate about details. Angie couldn't have shown up that night if she hadn't written down the date that mattered so much to Jenny and me.

Maybe empathy is as simple as remembering something that matters to someone you work with. I recorded my last two audio books in a small home studio in Nashville. The guy who runs it, Joe Loesch, is an audio master. He did such an amazing job. A year later, I saw him at an event but I didn't talk to him about the books or how great a job he did. I asked him instead about his dog, who had been ill the last time I was there. Joe and his wife love that dog and it's nearing the end of its life. Joe was honored that I remembered and cared enough to ask. I showed up to an important part of his life, his dog.

Empathy doesn't need to be big. (And it doesn't have to always involve dogs.) We're such a take society that even the littlest gift feels enormous.

Your coworkers need you to show up. Your clients need you to show up. Your vendors need you to show up. If you want them to show up when you do a Career Jump, plant empathy in your orchard. Show up in someone else's life first.

■ Make People Bigger

No one likes to feel small or insignificant or like everyone is laughing at them in their underwear during the weigh-in of their first wrestling match in the eighth grade. Hypothetically speaking.

People want to know we see their needs and we actually think they warrant attention. That's what empathy does. It makes people bigger.

I try to do this for most of my speaking engagements.

I have an agent who books gigs for me. They interact with the client, set up the whole thing and then e-mail me a dossier about the event. It's mostly just a PDF but dossier sounds like I might be a spy with a briefcase attached to my arm so let's go with that. I fly, meet the host, melt people's faces off with my ideas and then come home. But in just showing up like every speaker does, I miss out on something.

I miss the chance to be empathetic to the host and the people who attend the event.

That's why I try to have a fifteen- to thirty-minute phone call with the host before the event. During the call, I'll ask what their hopes are for the event, how I can serve the audience and what challenges I need to address. But the most unexpected question I ask and the most important one is this:

"A week after the event, what can I have done that makes you look like a rock star to the people who matter at your job?"

I often have to rephrase it a few times because speaking hosts aren't used to being asked that. They're actually a little taken aback. Instead of focusing on my needs, I just asked them "How can I make you bigger" and it surprises them. That's the question we need to ask if we want to know someone else's needs and how to act on them.

I promise, regardless of the specific career you have, you should ask the people you work with this type of question.

Ask clients: "What can I do to make you look like a rock star to your boss?"

Ask vendors: "What can I do to make you look like a rock star to your superiors?"

Ask your coworkers: "What can I do to make you look like a rock star to your manager?"

People will be taken aback by this, uncomfortably so, because it's the reverse of how so much of the workforce functions. That's just all the more reason to keep doing it.

How can we make another person bigger?

How can what I do make them bigger at work or give them a bigger opportunity or a bigger audience or a bigger belief in themselves?

It's the opposite of winning at someone's expense. It's putting someone's needs ahead of your own.

Doing this also helps me give a much better speech when I show up. People are often surprised at how much I know about the company and the challenges they are facing. I know both of these things not because I'm a genius but because I asked a few questions. I'm not a mind reader and neither are you, but that's one of the many benefits of empathy.

No one at work whom you make feel bigger will ever say, "That guy really made me feel better about myself. He really understood my needs and met them before I even asked. Fire him immediately!"

On the contrary, when things go awry, your boss will probably shout, "Get me Smith, he knows what I'm looking for!"

■ What to Do When Empathy Is Broken

You're not going to be perfect. Me either. There are going to be moments when instead of being empathetic we're just the opposite. We're selfish, foolish and dumb.

Instead of meeting someone's needs, we stepped all over them as we bullied our way to get our own needs met.

When that happens, and it will, the best thing you can do is to admit you were wrong.

When we make a mistake we want a villain to blame. We want someone to point the finger to other than ourselves.

As we discussed, you learn best from the failures you take responsibility for. You learn from the losses you own. And some of you reading this have lost, especially if you went through a Career Bump or hit a Career Ceiling. We can spend a lot of time and energy trying to assign blame. Time and energy that could have been applied to moving on, instead of staying stuck.

You also have to own things when you make a Career Jump. In the months after my last Career Do Over, I had to own that some of the relationships I lost, I lost because I had failed to invest in them in the first place. I had to own my narcissism and naivety in some situations. I had to own my foolish penchant for dramatizing what was essentially just me quitting a job, something thousands of humans do every day. I had to own my mistakes.

I don't put a lot of trust in people who can't say the words "I was wrong," or "I did that" or "I am sorry."

Nobody is perfect and people who pretend to be are lying. The interesting thing is that when you admit you were wrong or made a mistake to the people in your life, most of the time they already knew. The weaknesses you think you're revealing like a secret have been apparent to the people you work with for years. They've just been waiting for you to see them too. The craziest thing is that the thing we're afraid to lose by apologizing to coworkers—respect—is often what you end up gaining. Being honest earns you more respect from people than if you just pretend you have no faults.

Admit you were wrong. Apologize to anyone you weren't empathetic to. Own it so that you can start working on it.

▪ Starting with Chimney Sweeps, Ending with Dentists

I think in every book I've ever written, I've told a story about a dentist. The reason is that I go there often, given the torrid state of my mouth.

For this book, I had initially thought about including a section in hustle about the time I got a root canal one morning and then had to drive four hours to a speaking event that night. But that wasn't an example of hustle, that was an example of stupidity. At the bare minimum I should have asked someone to drive me there. (But I didn't really have anyone to ask, so maybe this is the ninety-second example that I'm not good at relationships.)

Fortunately, the dentist I go to stepped in with an example of empathy, allowing me to preserve my dental-story-in-every-book streak.

I had a dental appointment a few days after my most recent Career Do Over. Jenny and I were facing a rather uncertain financial future. Though the hope was that I'd be able to sign another book deal, the reality of that was months away from happening. We'd saved up money for a Career Jump like this but were aware we wouldn't be making any money for months to come.

A $2,000 dental appointment was going to be difficult on the old Acuff family budget. But I wasn't going in for teeth whitening.

This wasn't a "look-better appointment," this was a "fix some things so you get to keep your teeth" appointment.

During the visit my dentist asked me how things were going. I told him about my recent transition and described a little of what was going on. He listened quietly or as quietly as you can over the sound of a drill. He spent ninety minutes with me that day, doing a lot of work on three different teeth. As he wrapped up the appointment he patted me on the shoulder and said, "This one is on us today. You go figure out how to get back up on your feet."

I almost started crying in the chair, which is usually an activity I save for root canals. It caught me off guard. I wasn't expecting that and I left their office blown away by the entire situation.

It was an incredible act of generosity. But it was also an act of empathy, which we defined earlier as understanding someone else's needs and acting on them. You can't have generosity without empathy.

A lot of people might think that the dentist did something kind when he gave me the free dental care. He did, but the first kindness started with asking me how my life was and actually caring about my response. His willingness to waive my bill was empathy becoming generosity.

As long as I live in Nashville, I will never go to another dentist. I will tell everyone I know to go see him. I will forever be loyal to his business because of his generosity and empathy. A year later when my dentist asked me to attend an early morning fund-raising breakfast for a charity he supported, I couldn't wait to say yes. If he asks me to speak at an event for him someday, I'm going to say yes to that too. His empathy for me led to my loyalty to him, something every Career Jump will need at some point.

At times, empathy will feel complicated, but it's not. It only involves two things:

Understanding someone else's needs.

Acting on them.

Remember

- Empathy allows you to navigate the new relationships, new skills and new opportunities Career Jumps always bring.

- Knowing someone's story makes it difficult to judge, label or dismiss them. Seeing people for who they really are makes it a lot easier to work with them. Want more empathy? Know more stories.

- Care about what the people you care about care about. Figure that out faster by reading less minds and asking more questions.

- Empathy always makes people bigger, not smaller.

19

Be Present

In the skills section, I unveiled a dramatic new concept for having a great career. I called it "Go to work." It was a bit heady for some of us, a little ivory tower academic if you will, but at the end of the day I think we all agreed that whether we're working for someone else or ourselves, showing up for the job is probably important.

The trick, though, is you can launch a Career Jump and still be absent. You can have perfect attendance to whatever new opportunity you leap toward and still be missing. Being there physically, sitting in the seat as it were, is only one part of your Career Do Over. You still have to be present. Right now that's harder to be than ever because of all the distractions we're facing.

But, if you really want to reinvent your work and get ahead, there are three things you need to deal with—your phone, your computer and your meetings.

▦ Being Present with Your Phone

A friend once boasted to me that he had taken a break from his iPhone for thirty days. Before I could even clap for what sounded like an impressive feat, he clarified, "I didn't use my iPhone while I was in the bathroom for thirty days."

Wow, what's that, forty-two continual seconds of not using your phone? What clarity of mind and focus he must have gained in those moments. I hope he kept a diary about that experience and can turn it into a blog, if not a book, someday!

It's easy to laugh at things like that, but I'm not much better. I might not have phone conversations with strangers who don't know I'm at a urinal, but I've definitely checked Twitter from the bathroom. I've e-mailed people while jogging. Perhaps worst of all, I've started to look forward to red lights because it means I can get on my phone. Remember in the midnineties what people did when the light turned green? They just drove. I wish there was a horn that blared "Stop texting! Go! The light turned green!" that you could blow at obnoxious people like me.

We're becoming tethered to our phones much like the old ladies I saw the first time I went to a casino. I thought the experience would be glamorous like going to the Bellagio in Vegas. I wore a tie and walked through the door like a member of *Ocean's Eleven*. We were in Philadelphia, Mississippi, though, and the door we entered was in the nickel slot machines hall. We passed through rows of elderly women wearing necklaces that held their "casino cash cards," that were plugged into the machine. They were physically leashed to the slot machines, stuck. If I had an iPhone at the time I would have missed that moment, staring at my phone with my head down. My tether is not a casino necklace, it's a power cord.

I looked for a power outlet twice in the 1990s. Now, I scan airport terminals like an electricity junky. I judge the quality of a hotel room by the number of outlets it has. If there aren't some built into the lamp, I throw it out the window in a Def Leppard–like rage.

That's all ridiculous behavior, but our inability to be present because of our phones can threaten our relationships. Since you get the first gig via relationship and they're key to long-term career success, it behooves us to figure out how to be present with our phones. The easiest way, the quickest step you can take, is to quit "putting people on pause."

■ From Dinner Table to Conference Table, Locally Sourced Wisdom

One night, after our kids went to bed, Jenny and I were having a conversation. In the middle of it, I picked up my phone for the second or thousandth time that evening. I was probably shazaming a song, looking up the weather, replying to an e-mail, playing Plants vs. Zombies or tweeting about the amazing conversation I was missing because I was tweeting about it.

As I gazed longingly into the cool glow of my phone, Jenny said, "You just put me on pause. Let me know when you're ready to continue."

Spousal body slam!

She was right. By looking down at the phone in the middle of our interaction, I was telling her, "Pause right there for a second. There's something more important and more interesting than you that I want to focus on." And if I didn't have a phone, I would never do that. Can you imagine how the night would go if in the middle of talking to her, I reached my hand out, gently bopped her on the nose and said, "Pause. I'm going to think about football for thirty seconds. Feel free to keep talking but those words are going to roll right over me unabated by any sort of reply."

That would be a bad evening and a lot of us are creating bad days at work without even realizing it. When you're talking to co-workers about a project and you get lost in your phone, you just put them on pause. When you're meeting with your boss and you respond to an e-mail on your phone, you just told her she's not that important. When you're pitching a new client and you exit the conversation to check out your phone, you just put them on pause and told them you don't really want his/her business.

It's insane that we live in a world where just having one conversation at a time is considered a way to pay great honor to someone, but we do. If you want to be present with your phone and grow a better orchard, don't put people on pause.

▪ Be Present with Your Computer

When I worked for the Home Depot in the years before smartphones, which is all of history minus about twelve years, they blocked ESPN.com on all our work computers. I tried to figure out a way that knowing sports scores would help me write better advertising copy for curtains, but that was a difficult row to hoe. (Hang your curtains with A-Rod!) Unable to justify my need for access I instead just decided to be a jerk about the whole thing.

The audacity of that company to tell me I couldn't look at ESPN .com in their building, on their computer, on their dime.

Unfortunately, a lot of companies are acting just like the Home Depot these days. When they hire you for a particular role it's surprising how few times that role includes "Check Facebook incessantly." Very few job openings include, "Live tweet your day" in the list of responsibilities. And yet, it's so easy to act entitled to the wide swath of awesomeness that is the Internet.

That's why companies lose an estimated $6.5 billion during the fifteen-week fantasy football season.[1] And it's only going to get worse. The Internet is only going to get bigger and more interesting with more things to do that don't move us forward in our careers. Today is the smallest social media will ever be. Every day it expands.

To combat that siren's call, start by doing a time audit one day. If you have a job or work for yourself, write down every time you use the Internet for something non-work-related. Just keep a running tally of check marks; you don't have to write out what you were doing. If you have a hard time deciphering what's work related and what's not, just measure the number of times you'd have to do that lightning-fast browser close we all do when our bosses approach.

At the end of the day, or the week if you're feeling particularly energetic, tally the number. Now, tell me the value that all those non-work-related interruptions added to your job or your company. It's going to be anywhere from "zero to a nickel." Then tell me the number of times you'd like to review that list with your boss or clients. It's going to be anywhere from "zero to never."

If you're not happy with that math, if you find yourself checking more than you'd like, figure out how to break the cycle. For me, that means turning off WiFi when I write. I definitely use the

Internet for research, but research time is different than writing time. I have to disable the WiFi to get anything done.

Do work while you're at work. Novel concept.

▪ Be Present in Meetings

There are few things in life quite as exhilarating as having a meeting canceled. It's one of the best feelings you can have at a job. Everyone breathes a sigh of relief and says, "Oh, I just got an hour back in my day. Sweet joy." It's like a small pardon from a parole board.

It's possible that I'm biased about meetings, given how many I attended in my fifteen years of corporate work, but rarely have I heard someone say, "I wish I had more meetings to attend." Be that as it may, you're going to attend some during the course of your career. A lot probably. Knowing that, how do you make sure you're present in them? They might not matter to you at first glance, but if they matter to your company, boss and coworkers, they should. Here are a few tangible ways you can practice being present.

▪ Take Notes

Take notes on a piece of paper, with a pen. How quaint! Paper. Why such an old-fashioned approach? Because I've never scrolled through funny photos of llamas with weird haircuts on a piece of paper. I've never downloaded a few songs in the middle of a boring meeting with a piece of paper. I've never had to proclaim to everyone at the meeting, "I'm just using this paper for notes" as they stare at me, certain that I am using their meeting to catch up on e-mails. If you must go digital, an iPad or tablet is better than a laptop because at least then you have the accountability of people being able to see what you're doing. A laptop is too easy to hide behind the second a meeting gets dull. The notes don't have to be extensive either. You write down three lines and whoever is presenting is going to think you're an empathetic superstar. Showing up, part of skills, means showing up and being present. Plus, a week later, if someone has a question about the meeting, you'll have notes to refer to. Bonus.

■ Ask at Least One Question

The word "meeting" can mean anything from three people to three hundred, so adjust this advice accordingly, but asking one question will help you stay engaged. It forces you to focus on what is being presented. Asking good questions starts with listening to good information. You'll look like an idiot if you ask a question that someone else already asked. In addition to keeping you focused, a good question sends up a flare to everyone in the room that you're paying attention. Don't fake it if you honestly don't have anything to ask. But if you sit in a conference room for an hour of your life that you'll never get back and can't ask at least one question, you haven't tried hard enough. (Caveat: Don't be the person who asks fifty questions trying to impress the boss and making the meeting run late by thirty minutes. The goal isn't to impress your boss, that's just a side benefit. The goal is to be present, not showboat.)

■ Turn Your Phone Upside Down

Go all in on the meeting like a poker player, by putting your phone upside down on the table in front of you. Showing someone the back of your phone during a meeting is a neon sign that says, "I'm here! I'm present!" If you wear your phone on your belt, take it off and still put it on the table. Then burn that phone belt holster. Those are the business version of the fanny pack and are horrible.

This simple move will help you focus, because once your phone is on the table, to reengage with it means you have to tell everyone you're about to. The farther you put the phone away from you, the more obvious it becomes that you're about to check out if you try to pick it back up. We all think we're so sneaky checking e-mails under the table. We think we're under some sort of invisibility cloak when we do this. We're not. People see us and they know we're not present. Give yourself a fighting chance and flip that phone upside down. You could also leave it in your pocket unless it's one of those smartphones that are the size of a VCR. Last but not least there's the crazy option of just not bringing your phone with you to the meeting. Unless you're a heart surgeon who performs emergency transplants via text messages you can probably be away from your phone for a whole meeting. I promise.

While writing this section I thought to myself, "This is the most obvious advice ever!" And then I checked my phone four times. I even have to leave my phone in the kitchen when I go to bed so I can focus on sleep. If it's on my nightstand I can hear it calling to me. Plus, have you ever felt more rested after checking your e-mail right before bed? "Oh, look at all the things I failed to get done today! Now I feel peaceful."

In the years to come, being present at work is going to be game changing. No one is present anymore. But you and I should be. It doesn't make any sense to build a robust Career Savings Account and then throw it all out the window by not working when we show up for work.

Remember

■ Want to make sure you don't miss any opportunities during your Career Jump? Want to stand out at work? In a world growing increasingly distracted, do the wildly unusual and be present.

■ When you ignore someone you're face to face with for your phone, you've put him/her on pause and established that he/she doesn't matter. Be present to build better relationships.

■ If you're going to bother attending a meeting, don't be physically present and intellectually absent. Notes out, phone down, pay attention.

20

Never Jump Without Character

As a dancer shifts his position he keeps his balance. He does this by taking his center with him, he shifts his center of gravity, reestablishing his equilibrium in the very instant that he has leaped. Otherwise he will fall and hurt himself.
—MARY CAROLINE RICHARDS, *CENTERING IN POTTERY, POETRY AND THE PERSON*

You need character the most when you decide to chase a dream. Looking at the Do Over chart, this is the moment when we make a positive, voluntary decision to do something very different with our lives. This is the upper-right-hand corner, that moment when we dare to try something new.

We broke through some Career Ceiling with our skills and now find ourselves with the chance to do something we never would have expected. We're going to open a new company! We're going to change departments at our current company. More than just our attitudes, we're going to lean into a major career change. Time for some action. Balloons and fireworks!

The moment you decide to make any sort of change in your

career, you send other areas of your life into chaos. The bigger the change, the bigger the chaos.

Anyone who has ever moved for a job knows what this feels like.

My sister-in-law's husband accepted a new job near us in Nashville. They made a career decision. Suddenly, they needed to sell their house. They needed to find a short-term rental property he could live in while he worked in Nashville until their house sold. She had to quit her job. They had to say good-bye to all their friends in Auburn, Alabama. One decision, to take the job, kicked off a storm of chaos in nearly every area of their lives.

Character helps you navigate this chaos. Because no matter what happens, you can lean on your character. You might need to make new relationships in a new city. You might need to learn new skills at a different job. You might need more hustle than you initially thought humanly possible. Those three areas of your Career Savings Account might feel temporarily low during a Career Jump but your character won't be. Wherever you jump, your character jumps with you. I might have left some things when I jumped away from my last job, but I didn't leave me. I brought my brain, I brought my heart and I brought my character when I jumped.

And I needed them because I landed in the middle of chaos.

The bad news is that you can never completely eliminate the chaos in your life. That might sting at first, but once you realize chaos is not inherently good or bad, you can get more comfortable with it.

This book is a product of chaos.

I didn't plan to write a book about what it means to have a Do Over in your life. This exact book was not on some five-year plan I had. This was not simply the next book up on my list. When I jumped from my last job, I found out I needed my Career Savings Account to make the Do Over successful. In talking with other people I realized I was not alone in that need.

This is when I made a series of decisions.

I asked friends for literary agent recommendations.

I interviewed a few agents and hired one.

I wrote a book proposal.

I wrote a marketing plan.

I wrote the introduction to this book as a sample.

I wrote a detailed chapter-by-chapter outline.

Those were positive, voluntary decisions I made.

And then I submitted to the chaos.

What if I sent out the proposal and not a single publisher responded? What if spending three years essentially off the market had crippled my ability to attract other people who want to publish my books? What if outsiders thought the only reason my last books sold at all was because I worked for a company that had a large platform?

I had to form some new relationships. I had to admit that I didn't have all the skills I needed to run my own business yet. I had to hustle harder than I ever have before. A Career Jump often presents a terrifyingly accurate view into the true contents of your Career Savings Account. In the months that followed, I had to rely heavily on my character. I had to be generous with my time as I established myself in the marketplace. I had to be present to the moment. I had to be empathetic to understand the new people I would be working with.

I had to send out the proposal into what felt like chaos.

Which I did.

A few weeks later, publishers bid on my next two books.

We scheduled an auction.

A final bid was made.

More chaos ensued and it was wonderful.

Is living with the chaos of a decision easy? Not really, but you do get used to it. Over time, as you invest in character you develop a "chaos callus."

Jenny and I could not have risked what we risked with our last big Career Jump at the start of our marriage. We hadn't experienced any chaos. We had no precedent. We had not been stretched or tested in any other way. We were chaos rookies. Now though, years later, several moves later, we're OK with chaos. We don't create it for the sake of creating it. Correction, Jenny doesn't create chaos. I try to create it sometimes as a way to hide from something else I'm afraid of. I've discovered that's a lightning-fast way to drain a Career Savings Account. I didn't realize I did that until I did the exercises in this book.

When real chaos, not the fake kind I'm prone to manufacture, comes for Jenny and me, we don't fight it. If anything, we tend to lean into it, knowing that the words "easy" and "adventure" very rarely travel together.

Relationships built. Skills sharpened. Character strengthened. Doing those three things alone would make you stand out in the workforce, but the Career Savings Account has one final piece. Something that has the ability to exponentially multiply everything we've done so far.

It's time to hustle.

Investment 4
HUSTLE

How You Work

Career
Opportunity
(Hustle Investment)

Positive

Involuntary

Investment 4: Hustle

Music is in the piano only when it is played.

—JACK GILBERT

I believe you are capable of far more than you think.

I believe this because everyone I've ever met who hustled, discovered they were.

Part of this might be due to the fact that we tend to woefully underestimate our own capabilities, but the majority of the reason is because hustle is not just something we add to our Career Savings Account. It is something that multiplies everything else we have in it.

Lest we forget, the formula is (Relationships + Skills + Character) × Hustle = Career Savings Account. Hustle amplifies the collective sum of what we've worked on thus far.

Though at times it sounds like the name of an AXE body spray or a word you'd see plastered on the side of an energy drink, it's actually a lot less flashy than that. "Hustle" is simply shorthand for "work hard."

If relationships are who you know, skills what you do, and character who you are, hustle is how you work on each. If your career were a car, it would be the fuel. Without fuel, the most amazing car is a large, expensive, paperweight. Drive through a rural area, every

car stuck in someone's front yard is a career that the grass of inertia is reclaiming. Hustle refuses to allow that to happen.

Hustle amplifies relationships since frequency is the key to strong ones. Hustle is the reason you'll work hard to stay connected to the people who matter to you. It multiplies skills, giving you the push to learn new ones and the drive to sharpen old ones. It grows character because patience, generosity and empathy are not easy. Impatience, greed and selfishness take far less work, but hustle won't let you take the easy way out. When your work in one of the first three investments stirs up an unexpected opportunity, it will be hustle that meets it at the door.

Without hustle, you don't end up with a Career Savings Account, you end up with wasted potential. A cautionary tale like so many NFL draft busts. That number one quarterback didn't have to try that hard in high school. His natural talents carried him all the way through college without the need to hustle. But eventually, your talent either wanes or the competition catches up. Suddenly, being tall, fast and strong isn't enough. You actually have to work hard. You actually have to hustle.

The challenging thing about a fuel like hustle is that it can be misused. It's often thrown out as an excuse to step all over relationships: "I'm just hustling!" It's often the rallying cry of the most aggressive, annoying, self-promoting people we know. There is a thin line between hustle and hassle. It can also mutate into raging workaholism, making us hamsters on a wheel where we think more hustle is the solution to get somewhere. But spinning faster on a stationary object doesn't move us forward an inch. It just makes us muscular, exhausted hamsters, which is a terrifyingly specific thought. Busyness is not the same thing as hustle.

No, hustle needs the other components of the Career Savings Account every bit as much as they need it. If hustle is a fuel, skills are the gas tank. Skills focus hustle, allowing the fuel to be placed in the right place in the car for a long journey instead of just spraying the gas all over the vehicle directly from the hose with undisciplined actions that turn careers into smoldering bonfires, not modes of transportation. Relationships spur hustle on when it feels like quitting and slow hustle down when it feels like burning out. Character emboldens hustle with patience when the orchard feels like it will take forever and temper hustle with empathy when it threatens to step on everyone in its path.

In the right hands, applied the right way, hustle can be amazing.

What does it take to make sure that's how you apply it?

Grit, awareness and flexibility.

21

Grit Is a Choice, Not a Feeling

I didn't want to be selling insurance at 40, wondering
what it would have been like to do stand-up.
—STEVEN WRIGHT, COMEDIAN

Fear hates hustle. Nothing enrages fear like deciding to actually work hard. As long as you're just dreaming of reinventing your career, fear will ignore you. Fear loves daydreamers and can't stand day doers.

The 70 percent of Americans who feel disengaged from their jobs aren't fearful. They're unhappy, maybe even miserable, but they're not afraid. Fear does not bother the stuck because they're already out of the game. Apathy, entitlement, frustration, doubt— there's a swirl of negative emotions you feel when you've given up the dream that you might be designed to do more with your life. There's no need for fear to waste its time adding to that storm.

Fear would love nothing more than for you to have a host of relationships, character to spare and skills off the charts that you never put to use through hustle. Fear loves wasted potential and missed opportunities like I love queso. Hustle won't stand for it though. Hustle knows you have to do the work others don't to enjoy the results others won't. Hustle tries. Then it fails. Then it tries again, because of grit, which is simply being brave when you don't feel like being brave.

The problem is that grit is fun . . . to watch other people have.

When we think about things like grit, bravery and courage, we often imagine those moments from movies. A hero is up against impossible odds. It's difficult but he buckles down, gives his all and survives! At worst, he has to hold his breath under water or punch a few bad guys who were from the big corporation that was trying to steal his farm and/or dog. His girl, who is probably the brunette tomboy he ignored for the hot blonde all too long, will kiss him as the credits play.

Yay, grit!

We think grit is grimaces and grinding it out and wiping sweat off your brow as you save the day! We think it will feel great.

Here's the truth about grit:

Grit makes you feel like throwing up.

Grit feels like crying. A lot.

Grit feels like losing sleep.

I wish I were describing theory, but I'm not, I am describing large swaths of my life. Jenny and I didn't sleep that well during the first half of 2014. We had a lot of 3 A.M. brainstorm sessions. Have you ever had those? You roll over in the middle of the night and your spouse says, "Are you awake?" You reply, "I am, let's have a deep, detailed conversation about the situation we're facing and pretend it's not 3 A.M.!"

At one particularly challenging point, I almost started crying in a hipster coffee shop. A guy I used to work with asked me how it was going and I told him it was hard losing friendships. Out of nowhere I felt tears welling up. I started internally shaming those tears back down, "Be cool, Jon! Don't cry in front of the hipsters. Never let someone in skinny jeans see you cry! Force those emotions back down with sarcasm! No one puts baby in a corner." I realize that was all over the place but that's why it was internal.

That moment didn't feel great, but that's the thing about grit.

It's ugly and messy and not at all heroic-looking when it's really happening.

It's hard. Next time you feel like a coward because you're about to make a difficult decision and you feel like throwing up, don't beat yourself up. Next time you cry those tears that feel so stupid because you think brave people wouldn't, stop listening to that lie. Look at grit the right way. Grit never feels like bravery because it's not a feeling, it's a choice.

If you're going to make new relationships, you need to have grit.

If you're going to learn new skills, you need to have grit.

If you're going to have strong character, you need to have grit.

If you're going to hustle, you need to have grit.

Grit is being stubborn in the face of fear. Grit is the first time you try something and it's the thousandth time too. Grit is believing in *can* when *can't* is loud. Grit is expecting fear and moving forward anyway. As author Stephen Pressfield says, "The amateur believes he must first overcome his fear; then he can do his work. The professional knows that fear can never be overcome. He knows there is no such thing as a fearless warrior or a dread-free artist."[1]

If we could perfectly beat fear forever and then begin the process of reinventing our work, we wouldn't need grit. But that's not the way fear works. You're reading my fifth book and I experienced more fear about writing this one than any of the others. I didn't stop being afraid on book two or three, forever wiping my hands of an annoying mosquito I had squashed. If anything, I opened my home-office door to find fear had multiplied overnight into a swarm of bloodsuckers I had to wade through to get to my laptop. Which I did, because grit goes.

The first time you bump into hustle, an alarm goes off somewhere deep in the recesses of fear's mansion. Someone is storming the castle. Someone is daring to multiply everything they have in their Career Savings Account. And so fear walks calmly to the room that every bad guy in every movie has that is full of weapons. The doors are thrown open and two very big lies are removed from the wall. The lies become crippling questions that will deflate your sense of hustle before you've even left the front door. Here is what they are:

Question #1: What If I Don't Have What It Takes?

The only thing more exhausting than chasing a dream is running away from one. I ran from the idea of writing for years and the question that haunted me the most was, "What if I don't have what it takes?" The tradeoff I was making when I allowed this question to win was:

I would rather not try and not know I don't have what it takes, than try and know for certain.

It's a career twist on the question "Is it better to have loved and lost than to never have loved at all?"

This is a fascinating fear because as many times as we encounter it, we never take the time to dissect it. Let's unravel it for a minute.

What "It" do we mean by "what It takes?" What is the It? To be wildly successful? To be the greatest writer, business owner, chemist in the world? Our willingness to leave It undefined destroys us before we've even started. Of course we don't have what It takes, we don't even know what the It is.

If I define my "It" as writing books, then you bet I have what it takes. I've published four; I've already proven I can accomplish my It. If I leave It completely undefined, though, the fear gets to shift and morph the It into whatever discourages me the most on any particular day. During the writing of this book, fear tried to tell me the It I did not in fact have was "writing a book for a New York City publisher."

So now, because of the mailing address of my publisher, I've lost the ability to write books? That's ridiculous.

The trick is that our natural tendency is to think, "Well, then the solution must be that I have to know what my It is."

At which point fear shifts its focus and says, "Yes, that is true, you have to know exactly what your perfect purpose is and define your It to the nth degree. In fact, everyone else on the planet has already done this and it's too late for you."

Again, that's a lie. You don't need a perfect purpose to have a Do Over. In fact, if you don't know what your It is, building the Career Savings Account can shed some light on It. And if you already know what It is, your Career Savings Account will only make it easier to accomplish. (We'll jump deeper into why you need flexibility more than perfection when it comes to hustling on a dream later in chapter 23.)

There's also an unspoken time limit to the idea that "I don't have what It takes." When we say that, what we're really saying is "I will never have what it takes." Fear loves to take something true and add invisible words to turn it into a lie.

You might not have what it takes today. You might not have what it takes to run a business today, finish your college degree today or record an album today. But who said it had to happen today? Fear did.

Fear adds unseen time limits and expectations to our hustle moments. Instead of listening to fear, throw some grit back in its face. Instead of saying, "I don't have what it takes," say, "I have what it takes to try."

That's what we all have. Sixteen years ago, when I started writing professionally, did I have what it takes to write a business book? Nope. I didn't. But I did have what it takes to try learning how to be a writer. We all have what it takes to try. And trying is the only way you learn how to have what it takes anyway.

We all get to try. That's the beauty of a Do Over. That's the role of grit. It's simply the act of trying, and in many cases, trying again.

■ Question #2: What If I Pick the Wrong Thing to Hustle On and Miss My Opportunity?

The fear of missing out is one of the deadliest lies we listen to. It usually goes something like this in my head:

"I better say yes to this random opportunity. I feel like it might be the wrong one to work on, but what if I'm mistaken? What if this is the single most important opportunity I'll ever get? Is this the one that will break my entire career wide open? If I pass up this opportunity, some doppelgänger of mine, with less gray hair and better teeth, will say yes to it. He'll go on to fame, piles of cash and more success than the world has ever known. Friends and family will say, 'Why were you so dumb? Why did you say no to that? It's so obvious.' I'll hang my head low and sit in a dark, moldy room forever muttering about what could have been while I grow one of those awkward neck beards."

In moments like that, I feel as if I am standing in front of a wall of combination locks. I am missing only one number to unlock the entire wall, leading to a stress-free life full of bliss. Every new opportunity is someone holding up a piece of paper with a number on it. What if I say no and miss the piece of paper that has the final number on it?

When that fear comes up, I either hide from all opportunities, paralyzed that I'm going to say or do the wrong thing, or I say yes to any opportunity that crosses my field of vision. You've got a podcast that records at midnight, an audience of mostly relatives and you want me to record it during my family vacation? Done! Then, to disguise my fear, I tell people I say yes to some things because I like to serve people and help other dreamers who are just like me. Somewhere in this twisted hair ball of fear that is my heart is some degree of truth about wanting to help people. But more than anything, I say yes all the time because I'm terrified of what I might miss.

I think this stems from the fact that we like to believe in the concept of "once-in-a-lifetime opportunities." If we were honest, we'd call these what we really hope they are: "Win-the-lottery moments." We believe in these types of opportunities often out of laziness. The picture of having your entire life changed in the course of one unexpected, outrageous experience sure beats actually working hard. The grit years are not fun to talk about; it's far better to have Richard Branson run into you at a Whole Foods and give you a billion dollars of start-up for your business while you shop for complicated olive oils. That's a better story, but once-in-a-lifetime opportunities happen a lot less than we think.

A twenty-three-year-old entrepreneur told me he was facing a once-in-a-lifetime opportunity. He felt overwhelmed and under a lot of pressure. I told him that he did have a great opportunity on his hands but it wasn't a once-in-a-lifetime opportunity. He had fifty years of life left. Imagine at twenty-three feeling like you'd experienced your only once-in-a-lifetime opportunity. What do the next five decades of life look like, just reminiscing over that one opportunity? Living in the wake of that?

Working for Dave Ramsey was a great opportunity, but it wasn't once in a lifetime in the way we like to define things. They talked to me about a job in 2008, but the fit wasn't right. I said no the first time. We talked again in 2009 and decided against it. It wasn't until 2010 that I decided to join the team, which was I guess my "thrice-in-a-lifetime opportunity."

Were there elements that were unique and might not ever happen again in my lifetime? Definitely, but beware the temptation to apply the once-in-a-lifetime label to every opportunity you face.

Missing the right opportunity is half the fear we'll deal with and the other is picking the wrong opportunity. For me, the question I hear when I'm afraid of hustling on the wrong thing is:

"What if the career I've chosen is just a fad, like swing dancing?"

Fear uses that particular activity against me because of a girl I once knew. I met her during my last year of college before I dated

Jenny. At the time, swing dancing was all the rage. I think the movie *Swingers* was out at the time and Big Bad Voodoo Daddy was gigantic. You are not going to believe the second half of this sentence, but it felt like everybody was into swing dancing.

Every Wednesday night I went to a place called Five Points with my friends for Swing Dance night. After a few weeks, there was a girl there who I always danced with. We never dated—dance was about the only thing we had in common—but for a few months we were consistent partners. This is starting to sound like the plot of a movie: a preppy girl meets a boy from the wrong side of the street and swing dancing teaches them they are not that different after all.

One night, as we swung or did whatever is the past tense of the verb "to swing-dance," she told me she had quit her job. Her parents were against the decision but she was going full time into swing dancing. I smiled and nodded while trying to flip her over my head, but inside I was thinking, Does she not know this is a trend? This nightclub is already a little emptier than it was two months ago. We're on the tail end of this adventure. Swing dancing won't last forever.

In her passion to launch a Do Over, she missed the very obvious signs that swing dancing wasn't a great foundation to build her life on. Why didn't she work on a small skill, like learning how to be an instructor at night while she still worked her day job? Why did she gamble everything? I never asked her and we lost contact, but fifteen years later, I still think about that conversation, especially when I'm afraid.

What if I've just chased the equivalent of swing dancing with my life? What if speaking, social media and being an author are all the rage right now but will eventually cool off? What if you can't be a full-time author any more than you can be a full-time swing dance instructor?

I know that fear is stupid. People have been full-time authors for centuries. Being an author isn't a new thing. Social media and the

Internet will change in the years to come, but they won't go away. If anything, they're only going to get bigger. And you can be a full-time author just like you can be a full-time swing dance instructor, if you pursue both the same ways. With small skills, big patience and hustle.

I was a professional writer for fifteen years before I tried my latest Career Jump. This was no impulsive leap upon hearing the first siren call of the writer's life. But fear is still loud. Eventually, though, I learned a simple lesson for when it shows up.

Fear is not the same thing as regret.

Sometimes we confuse the two as if they are the same, but they are not. They are very different.

Regret has a much longer shelf life than fear. Fear is a moment, a beast of a decision you're afraid to make, a demon of a day you're afraid to face. Regret is much more of a slow burn. If fear is a tidal wave, large and loud and temporarily very powerful, regret is a small stream that cuts a canyon into your heart slowly over time.

Change isn't easy. Do Over moments are not always simple. I know that. I hate them sometimes in my own life. I get afraid but I have to choose something and so do you.

Fear or regret?

Will you face the fear of today or the regret of forever?

I don't know what happened to my swing dance partner, but she had grit. She tried. Could she have done it differently? Sure, we can always look back on some Career Do Over and see something we could have done another way. For all I know, she taught swing dancing for a year full time and then tried something else. Why do I let fear hold her up as the poster child for failure, as if choosing the wrong opportunity at twenty-two years old forever crippled that woman's career?

We get a choice: fear or regret.

Will you attack your fear of failure, maybe even fail and try again? Cleaning the beach of your life after a wave that crushed you but left lesson upon lesson in its wake?

Or will you give up on your Do Over? Believing that kids can dream but adults must settle? Allowing that thin line of regret to trickle over time until it splits your life in half?

I choose fear. I choose grit.

Let the waves come.

■ Make Grit Decisions

If grit is stubbornness in the face of fear, how do we actually make decisions that reflect that? Wave metaphors are nice, but what does that look like on a Sunday night when you've got an opportunity to change jobs? What does that look like when you're faced with a career choice that's not easy? How do you move forward today and not regret the option you picked someday? How do you make grit decisions?

Here is what every grit decision needs:

■ Time

We think the word "hustle" has to mean fast, but it doesn't. Hustle can also mean focus, it can also mean intention, it can also mean pace. The only way you can make grit decisions is if you give them the time they need. Though there will be sprint moments in any career, a year from now when you look back on a decision you made, you'll want to know that you gave it the time it really deserved. Don't confuse hustle with rush.

▪ Counsel

Lean on your relationships. Some of the worst decisions are made alone. If the only counsel you're keeping is your own, you're going to make some isolated choices. Who are your advocates? What have they said about the opportunity you're facing? Have you given them time to reflect on it or are you rushing right by the wisdom they have to offer? You don't have to wait for perfect consensus from everyone you know before you make a move. As Arthur Goldberg noted, "If Columbus had an advisory committee he would probably still be at the dock." But don't hide the decision you're trying to make from the people you trust. Let them speak into it. A year from now, looking back on the decision, you'll be glad you made it as a team. If you doubt a decision later, they can remind you why you made that choice since they were part of it.

▪ Questions

Always ask awesome opportunities, awesome questions. In our fear that something is too good to be true, we often don't ask the decision in front of us hard-enough questions. We skimp on due diligence, so eager to jump and make a decision that we end up ignoring obvious warning signs. Every bad decision I've ever made has one thing in common: I thought it was a good decision at the time. Give your counsel the chance to ask you hard questions by asking them one of your own. I tell my advocates about an opportunity I'm struggling with and then say, "What am I not seeing right now?" I know that despite my best intentions and ability, there's a side to every story I am missing. Got a great opportunity? Ask it great questions.

▪ Kindness

Give yourself permission to make the wrong decision, because guess what? You're going to. You're going to pick the wrong thing sometimes. You're going to give your decisions time, get counsel, ask lots of good questions and still choose incorrectly. So am I. You never bat 100 percent when you reinvent your career. We jump to the wrong job. We develop a skill that our industry stops valuing. We move our family across the country for a job that falls apart in six months. Break the tension of feeling like you're going to be perfect by giving yourself some kindness from the outset.

▪ Honesty

The worst part of regret is that when we look back on a decision, we lie to ourselves. Equipped with the kind of information only hindsight can provide, we beat up our former selves for their stupidity in making the wrong decision. That person in the past, the you from before, didn't know what you know now, though. They couldn't have predicted that the boss who hired you for a new job would leave that job, stranding you with a new boss who didn't like you. You're not a mind reader. Be honest about that. When you look back on a decision, remember that you made that decision with the best information you had at the time.

▪ Build a Grit List

The good thing about reinventing your work is that once you do, you never have to do things you don't like again. You'll be like one of those people who have dream jobs and get to spend 100 percent

of their days on passions. You'll probably sail to the Galapagos Islands to study tortoises and have one of those Instagram accounts we all love/hate to follow. Just one sunset and tortoise after another as you enjoy the perfect life.

Only you know that's not true. There's no such thing as a perfect job. There's no job where you get to do only the things you love doing. Those don't exist. As a doctor told me, "In every job, there's a rectal exam."

You're going to need a "Grit List," a collection of things you hate doing but are critical to your career. I said "hate," although my mother always told me that was a horrible word and I should instead say, "I do not prefer cauliflower."

But we're not talking about eating albino broccoli right now. We're taking about hustle. About shaping our Career Savings Accounts in such a way that we're ready to capitalize on unexpected opportunities. We're talking about digging in our heels, buckling down and doing all the little things that add up to big careers. We're talking about grit.

There will be tasks, projects and activities you have to do in your career that you hate. No matter which stage you're in—a Career

Ceiling, Career Bump, Career Jump or Career Opportunity—you'll have to do some things you don't love. You might not have to do as many later on in your career as you become established, but there will never be a time when you only do the things you like.

That's why we all need a Grit List, a short list of the skills we grit our teeth and do regardless of how we feel. Instead of trying to trick ourselves into liking them, we admit we hate them, recognize the value of them and then commit to do them.

The Grit List is where we'll put some of the necessity skills we have to learn in order to have a Do Over. We initially picked a curiosity skill in Chapter 13 as the first new skill to focus on in order to build momentum. Now that we've built some, it's time to find a skill we have to do. Since hustle is fuel, this is our chance to apply some energy to a skill we might not love doing.

E-mail is on my Grit List.

I can't stand doing e-mail. It's never done. Every time I do it and feel good about emptying it out, it refills itself. I hate saying no to things (see fear of missing out, above), and every e-mail feels like a chance for me to fail. I'm not very organized (see missed flight from Los Angeles), and the folders are overwhelming.

After years of trying to fall in love with e-mail using systems and apps and methods and all manner of technology to beat it back into submission, I am resolved that we hate each other. That's OK. But guess what? My job requires e-mail.

Responding to e-mail is part of what it means to be a modern writer. Maybe if I were in my late eighties and called computers "the computer machine," I could avoid ever using them. But I can't. I'm too young to make a play for pigeons as my mode of communication. Ponies stopped expressing long ago.

So I admit I hate it and put it on my Grit List. Then I recognize the value. My inbox isn't just full of data. There are relationships in there. There are skills in there. How I respond to people reflects on my character. I don't get to say, "I want to invest a lot in relationships, but not via one of the most popular ways people communicate today." I also get to hustle on unexpected opportunities if I stay on top of my e-mail. I got to speak to one of the teams at Comedy Central because I responded to an e-mail from one of their executives.

On my Grit List I wrote the value of e-mail (new opportunities, stronger relationships, chance not to be a Luddite, etc.). Then I commited to do it. I don't need to love it to get it done. I just need to do it. With grit.

It's like running. Some people love it. The very idea of doing it makes them smile and they bound out the front door with glee on their face. I do not like running, I like being done with running. I like the feeling I get after, not before. I like my pants fitting. In order to run regularly, I recognize the value of it, put it on my Grit List and then do it.

What skill would you put on your Grit List? Is it e-mail like me? Or is there an invisible skill from Chapter 10 you'll need grit to master?

Is dealing with vendors at work on it? You love doing design work but can't stand the printing process. Paper samples, price quotes, figuring out the exact number of brochures to get printed and press checks are your nightmare. In the connected Internet age, the idea that you have to drive to the print shop to physically check the print run drives you crazy. Time to admit that's part of your job. Time to admit the best way to produce the best print pieces is to check samples onsite. It has value.

Is budget season the worst part of your job? You can't stand balancing all those numbers, trying to predict your costs and revenue next quarter? Put budgeting on your Grit List. Acknowledge that if you don't work hard on your budget, your team won't get any money allotted for projects next year. And teams that don't have budgets or projects don't have reasons to be employed for very long. Thus, even though you might feel overwhelmed or afraid to sit down with next year's budget, you can see the critical value of that activity.

Fear and frustration are coming. They're a consequence of actually doing something meaningful with your career.

If this book was titled *How to Stay the Same,* we wouldn't have to address grit. But it's not, it's titled *Do Over* and those are scary. That's OK. We all get scared. That's part of the price of reinventing your career. Most people won't pay it.

Don't be most people. Go with grit.

Remember

- Relationships get you the first gig. Skills get you the second. Character prepares you for any outcome. Hustle allows you to make the most of the whole process.

- Hustle takes grit.

- Grit is a choice, not a feeling. Don't wait until you feel brave to hustle. Choose to hustle until you feel brave.

- You'll never know you have what "It" takes until you define "It" and then try "It."

- Regret has a longer shelf life than fear. Face the fear of today instead of the regret of forever.

- Grit decisions take time, counsel, questions, kindness and honesty.

22

Hustle Has Seasons: Use Awareness to Recognize Them

I often get e-mails like the one Bob S. sent me:

> What do you do when 5 AM is already the time you get up to go to work and your work is an hour away? At what point do you hustle? I have a little free time at lunch, but I find it hard to dive into writing or anything else when I know that I have to be back in an hour or less.
>
> I get home about 5:30 PM most days and it's go go go until the kids are in bed at 8:30 PM (more like 9 to 9:30 but I didn't want to seem like a bad father). Once they're in bed is the only time my wife and I get to talk . . . Even if I write at that point, she likes me in there with her so the TV is on while I write and I can't concentrate.
>
> There's obviously some times where I'm not hustling and I could be, playing Madden on a Friday night, watching TV, etc. If you're mentally

> beat from your week (10 hours between work and driving every weekday) it's hard to focus without falling asleep.
>
> Any suggestions you have will be met with action on my part.

Bob is doing everything he can to hustle. He might be able to carve out a sliver during lunch or focus more on the weekends, but unless he's playing eight hours of Madden every Friday night, he's already running pretty thin. He's not suffering from a lack of effort, he's missing awareness, the second principle of hustle.

Awareness is critical because like relationships, not all hustle is created equally.

▪ Hustle Has Seasons

Every investment in the Career Savings Account requires you to navigate some degree of tension. At different times in your career journey you'll have to hold two opposite thoughts in your head at the same time. For instance, in character we talked about how whenever you're dealing with people, the mantra, "It's not personal, it's just business," falls apart. Everything we do has personal consequences that must be informed by our character. But at the same time, you'll have to work hard not to take the decisions other people make too personally or emotion will rule the day. We discussed that the secret to empathy is believing that everyone is the same. We all have common hopes and needs. At the same time, we're also unique with very different career dreams. Two very opposite things are true and so there's tension.

Hustle, though, has the greatest collection of tensions of all the investments you'll make. You have to work incredibly hard but also rest. You have to say yes to a lot of opportunities but also protect your time and say no regularly. You have to have grit to hold on in tough times and flexibility to quit when it's time to move on. The specific tension you'll face with awareness is that you have more time than you think and you have less time than you think.

Bob from the e-mail was looking for a treasure trove of unused time. Perhaps an eighth day that high-achieving people have secretly been using for hundreds of years, but there's not one. Instead, there are seasons. There are different times in your life, career, year and week when you will hustle differently than in others.

Trying to hustle in the wrong season ruins the other parts of your life. Take something ordinary like vacation as an example.

Have you ever tried to go on vacation during the middle of a big work project? It was prescheduled, you couldn't move it, and so despite the fact that your job is blowing up you head to Florida for a few relaxing days. Only they're not. You're constantly checking e-mail. You're sneaking in conference calls as your husband waits to walk to the beach. You might be miles away from work, but your head is still in the building.

You end up ruining the vacation and not providing much quality input to the project too. You don't return home rested, you return home feeling like a failure. Neither part of your life, vacation or work, got the best of you. The reason this happened is that you didn't have any awareness and hustled during the wrong season.

That week of vacation wasn't the time for you to get ahead. It was supposed to be a vacation, but your expectation that it could be both broke both. So perhaps the very first question you need to ask as you prepare to hustle on reinventing your work is the one that will lead to greater awareness: "What season am I in?"

Maybe right now you're in "med school" season. That's what a friend who is in his early twenties calls the hustle he's putting in at his start-up. He's working seventy-hour weeks, hustling as hard as he can to get a new company off the ground. He felt a little guilty about that until he started calling this season of his life med school. If he was learning to be a doctor, no one would tell him, "I think you're working too hard. You're always hustling. You need to take it easier on yourself. It's just medical school. Why are you studying so hard?" We as a culture understand that medical school requires intense, all-consuming hard work. Perhaps that's the season you're in with your hustle. It's sprint time. (If that is the season you're facing, make sure it has a conclusion. Even doctors eventually graduate. Don't act like medical school is a twenty-year process and a speed you can maintain forever.)

Perhaps right now you're in "family season." You've got young kids and need to focus on establishing your family. A dad of a four-week-old told me he was still getting up at 5 A.M. to try to work on his dream. I told him to stop that. He was already getting up at 3 A.M. to help feed the baby. He had enough dream to work on right now, it was called "raising a human." That's plenty for that season.

You could be in the "pay-off-debt season." Maybe right now, your hustle is simply digging out from financial or career mistakes you made along the way. It's not fun, it's not easy, but being faithful to your commitments today will allow you to do more dreaming tomorrow. Don't feel guilty that you're not doing enough hustle on a dream you have right now. Go with grit. Keep your word. Finish what you started so that you can start new things eventually.

Hustle is often hard because we apply it to the wrong season. Bob felt that way until he realized what season he was in. There's great peace in knowing where you are and what you should be doing. Get a sense of which season you're in and then start to do the second part of awareness: focus.

▨ Hustle Is a Scalpel

I believe you are capable of far more than you think.

I also believe that in order to do more of what you are capable of you will have to do less of what you've been doing. That's what is counterintuitive about hustle. We tend to think it only means addition. We add new relationships, new skills and new character to our lives through the means of hustle.

That's the first half of hustle and the one most people get stuck on. You already feel busy and then you read a book that shames you into thinking you're not doing enough. There's more you can be doing. You have to hustle! Feeling this pressure you stuff your already overpacked life with more commitments and more activities. We mistakenly think that having greater awareness means adding greater amounts of activity to our lives. How did Bob end his e-mail to me?

"Any suggestions you have will be met with action on my part." We tend to think adding more action is the solution.

The first half of hustle is addition, but you don't get to add anything to your life unless you remove something else. Hustle isn't simply doing more. Greg McKeown wrote a brilliant book called *Essentialism* that focuses on "the disciplined pursuit of less." In it, he shares a philosophy Dieter Rams, the lead industrial designer at Braun, the consumer product company best known for electric razors, created: "Less but better."[1] That's what hustle is, doing less but better, which is why we need awareness.

Take out the skills and relationships note cards you wrote or the list you put in your notebook. Find one skill or one relationship that you think is critical to your Career Savings Account. In order to pursue either one of those, you'll need to find space in your life.

To find space you will need to pause, stop or reconfigure something else in your life.

I sometimes run the Nashville Marathon in the spring. I can't train for one in the fall, though, because I travel so much with my speaking schedule. I don't stop running in the fall, I'm still able to sneak some runs in with gritted teeth, but I put my training on pause to focus on other commitments.

I like to write first thing in the morning when my energy is highest. When I wanted to join a mastermind group of other businessmen who can challenge me, I had to stop writing at 7:30 A.M. every Tuesday. Meeting with the guys really matters to me and so I stopped something else so I can focus on that.

When my kids stopped taking afternoon naps I had to reconfigure my writing schedule. They were awake and I wanted to be able to spend time with them. That was a big part of why I started writing in the mornings in the first place.

Let's not pretend, though, that using hustle like a scalpel is fun or easy. We're too deep into this book to sugarcoat. Sometimes it's really hard and someone else in your life will need to point out some hustle you need to reconfigure.

One day I called Jenny from California and told her about a new speaking event I'd been offered. I said, "This will cover us financially for that month." She replied, "You're saying yes to too many things. We're already fine for that month. We're fine."

"Right," I replied, "but now we're finer." Jenny was quiet for a second and then said, "Well, then keep hustling and only saying yes all the time to every new opportunity. Just make sure you can earn enough money to buy a new family because this one won't still be around."

Noted.

She didn't say it with anger. It wasn't an argument so much as it was a scalpel moment. In my desire to hustle I was spinning out of control. I was saying yes too often to opportunities during a season when I needed to say yes to my family more. Plus, my wife was right, I've never won the Super Bowl or landed a plane on the Hudson. I wasn't getting the kind of speaking fee that would make buying a whole new family financially feasible. Far better to keep the one I currently have and hustle on what it means to be a good dad and a good husband.

That's hustle, a continual cycle of pause, stop and reconfigure.

Be proactive about doing that in your own life. Work on your sense of awareness. Don't wait for someone you love to call you out.

▨ Head Down, Head Up

Steeve G. doesn't wear an Oxford hoodie because he visited the famed university in England and found the gift shop prices to be fair.

He wears it because he has four master's degrees from Oxford. Born in India, Steeve spent two and a half years acquiring his degrees in England in astrophysics, computer science, mathematics and philosophy. I misspelled mathematics the first time I wrote that sentence in this book, that's how bad I am at math.

Since then, Steeve's moved to Raleigh, North Carolina, part of the Research Triangle, to work on his PhD.

In the course of our first conversation, I asked him when he would complete his PhD. He smiled and said, "Well, I thought it would be in a year or so from now, but I have to start over." At the sound of these words, my ears perked up.

"What do you mean, start over?" I asked.

"I was working on a problem, the core of my PhD, and discovered that the results I was going to get for this problem were not the results I wanted. I had to backtrack to see which of the assumptions I built the problem with were incorrect. I found that two of my assumptions were wrong and if I continued down that path, the final results would be too. So I have to start over."

"How long had you been working on the problem?"

"Twenty-two months," he said.

That Steeve was able to answer that question without weeping was astounding to me. I've worked with developers who spent a week working on some code that didn't work at the end of the week and they wanted to punch someone they were so aggravated at the time wasted. Steeve spent twenty-two months of his life on a single problem and needed to start over.

"What are you going to do now?" I said.

"I'm going to continue to play out the problem with the incorrect assumptions because I'm curious to see what happens. But I'm going to fix both of those assumptions and try again. If I don't, what's the point? This experiment could significantly help our understanding of matter. I have to fix it for it to help people at all."

There were two things about Steeve's story that struck me.

The first is that he changed the narrative of his Do Over moment. Perhaps his outlook is commonplace in the scientific community but most professions don't look at similar situations that way.

He didn't fail. His assumptions were incorrect.

He wasn't a failure. His results weren't the ones he wanted or expected.

He wasn't going to quit. He was going to launch a Do Over.

The problem is that most of us don't take the time to look at our lives that way. When we find ourselves in a job we don't like, what do we say?

"I hate this job. The people here are horrible. My boss is a jerk. The work is boring. They don't appreciate me. The culture is bad. I'm not doing the kind of work they promised me I'd be doing when they hired me."

Over and over we find a way to place the blame squarely on other people and other circumstances. It's not our fault, it's theirs. What if instead, though, we approached the situation like Steeve? What if, upon finding ourselves stuck we admitted, "The results I'm going to get if I stay here are not the results I wanted or expected. I need to backtrack and see which of my assumptions were incorrect. Did I expect this job to be something it never would be?"

Owning our part in the situation is often not fun, but maybe it's because we have the narrative all wrong. Lifting your head, admitting you're stuck and owning something doesn't mean you're a failure, it might just mean you took the wrong path and need to find a new one. When Steeve hit a ceiling, he didn't quit impulsively or get frustrated. He grabbed a new hammer and started breaking through it with a different mathematical approach.

This is certainly easier to type in a book than it is to do in real life, but it can be done.

The second thing about Steeve's story that struck me is that in addition to lifting his head to have awareness of where he is headed, once he realized that, he put his head down and got back to work. That's the final tension of awareness. Keeping your head down and hustling on the work, raising your head and making sure you're going in the right direction.

Awareness requires both and allows us to see the transition between seasons.

Snow skiing in just a bathing suit might make for an interesting postcard but if you do it every day, you're an idiot. The seasons have changed. If all you wear is a bathing suit when it's twenty below, you'll get sick. Awareness helps us recognize that the seasons have changed. When he found his research headed down an unexpected path, Steeve had entered a new season of hustle. Without awareness he might have never known.

Today, ask yourself: Is the work I'm hustling on right now going to lead to where I want to go? You don't have to know the exact path, because nobody does, but are you roughly headed in the right direction? If you want to be a musician and you're a pharmaceutical rep working seventy hours a week, not playing any music, stop kidding yourself. That path doesn't lead to music. If you've spent the last five years dreaming about going back to college but haven't taken a single class, stop pretending a diploma will magically land in your mailbox.

Look down at what you're hustling on, look up at where you want to go.

Hustle with awareness; without it, all the hustle in the world just gets you to the wrong place faster.

Remember

- Hustle takes awareness.

- Hustle has seasons. If you're in "med school" right now, put in the long hours. If you're not, make sure you're not neglecting other important commitments.

- Hustle is a scalpel. Use it to remove things from your life, not just to add things.

- Keep your head down and your head up. Hustle is about focus, not frenzy. Make sure you're headed in the right direction by doing regular temperature checks.

23

Career Yoga

You have more control of your life than you think. You also have a whole lot less than you think. That's tension number 4,342 you'll run into as you hustle.

Your day won't go according to plan unless you spend time planning it. The minute you start to live it, though, outside forces will conspire to make sure the plan isn't executed perfectly. I can write the greatest speeches I'm capable of. I can get amazing testimonials, clips of me doing what I do and sharpen my skills for years. The client still might go with a magician instead of me. I can't compete with that. I have next to no access to rabbits, especially since I don't have a falcon.

No, our careers rarely go according to plan. Don't believe me? Tell your baby that you have a huge presentation at work today. They will interpret that as the perfect time to throw up on whatever you're wearing for your big moment. Tell the project you're hustling on that you thought of every detail. The ship from China that has your product on it will get delayed by a hurricane that you apparently don't control.

In moments where we feel out of control, we often assume the solution is to hustle harder. To buckle down with more intensity. To clinch our fists tighter around the opportunity, but what if the answer was just the opposite? What if the secret to hustle was to have an open hand? To work as hard as we can, to be diligent and deliberate but not be crushed when things don't go perfectly? To instead, hustle with flexibility?

That's the biggest tension of hustle, working as hard as you can for results and then admitting you have less control over them than you think. That takes flexibility in a few key areas.

■ Be Flexible with Your Dream

Ever feel like you don't know exactly what you want to do with your life? Know who else feels that way? Everyone.

We think we have to know before we go, that we have to figure our lives out before we hustle, but the opposite is actually true. Purpose is often a by-product of hustle, not a prerequisite.

The more you hustle, the more skills you develop, the clearer what you thought you wanted to do becomes. I believe in having a fuzzy vision, not a perfect plan. A general direction you want to head that becomes clearer as you actually work on it. Perhaps you're the creative opposite of me; you love numbers. Math is your playground. With a business degree you could see yourself one day being a CFO. That's a fuzzy, faraway vision that you can work on. You can't tell what it would really involve because you're so far away from it at the beginning of your Do Over. But you hustle, knowing that the character, skills and relationships you develop will serve you in the long run.

Midway up the career ladder, as you get closer to that position, though, the realities of it become clearer. Maybe the CFO at your company has to work seventy hours a week. She has to spend a lot of time wooing investors, something you'd hate. The more time you spend in the industry, the more exposure you have to other CFOs. Maybe being a CFO means traveling constantly. You couldn't have possibly seen what it meant to be a CFO until you spent time hustling toward that fuzzy vision. Life is dreamed in big leaps and revealed in small steps.

Recognizing that it's not the position you thought it was, like Steeve and his mathematical equation, you respond with flexibility. You take a side path in a different direction, equipped with a robust Career Savings Account and new knowledge about something you don't want to be. You don't quit pursuing your love of numbers and instead become a painter. You still have grit, but flexibility allows you to shift the destination you're headed toward now that you really saw what the CFO destination looked like.

I never thought I'd shift to being a full-time author. That was never in the cards for me. I was a company man through and through, or at least I thought so. In 2004, I had a meeting with a friend I was trying to persuade to hire me full time. When I told her I'd like to work for her company, without hesitation she said, "We'd never hire a guy like you, you're an idea guy. You don't need to be at one company. You need to work at a bunch."

That was brilliant advice that I promptly ignored, doing everything I begged you not to do with wise advice you receive from your friends. I was inflexible with my hustle and didn't want to admit that I might be wired to be an author. I spent the next nine years working at companies.

Along the way I started to freelance on the side of my Home Depot job and I found out I liked it. I spent years building a healthy freelance client base and started to explore the reality that I might not be a company guy. In 2010, when Dave Ramsey offered me a full-time position, they asked me to focus on their company and not freelance. I closed my business and told my wife I would work for Dave for ten years. I told her that I'd finally found the company I'd be at for a long time. She laughed.

I didn't understand why Jenny laughed until I spent three years working for an entrepreneur. I realized I'm one too, only I don't want to create a business, I want to create ideas and books. My dream was changing but I didn't want to be flexible with it. I had a specific definition of it in my head and refused to be flexible. But the more I hustled, the more I realized I was an entrepreneur. The more that vision clarified. Finally, I had to be flexible with my dream and accept that I'm an author. Will I do what I'm doing right now forever? Maybe not, but for now being flexible with my hustle means working on my own.

You'll have to be flexible with your dream too. It's going to change in ways you can't begin to predict.

▪ The Work You End Up Loving Might Not Even Exist Yet

I told my sister, who is fifteen years younger than me, that when I was her age, what I'm doing now didn't physically exist. I spend a good deal of my day interacting with social media. I tweet. I post on Facebook. I pin images. A large part of my focus is interacting with my community online. Fifteen years ago, when I was twenty-three, that wasn't possible. Not for lack of effort on my part, but just that there was no Twitter. There was no Facebook. Blogs were in their baby stages and couldn't easily be updated. Imagine if I had sat at my kitchen table and thought to myself, "I need to figure out my dream."

Is it possible that I would have been able to conceive the invention of Twitter? Might I have daydreamed up Facebook? What then? Would I just wait for Mark Zuckerberg to invent it? Me and my Moleskine notebook, writing: "I hope there's a talented developer and two gigantic twins who are fighting over an idea right now that will one day be where I hustle." That's ridiculous. The same goes with picking a college major. When I was in college, almost nothing I'm doing now was a reality. I didn't get my first e-mail address until I was a junior. And I thought it wouldn't take off! I remember sitting in a computer lab, staring at a black and green e-mail screen thinking, "This is so dumb. Why would anyone ever do this?" This is probably the origin story of my hatred for e-mail.

I hope college students pick the major that's best for them, but they have to know the future is going to change what they do and how they do it. You've got to be flexible with your dream because it might not exist yet.

■ Your Dream Will Change Over Your Lifetime

I had a fuzzy vision in the third grade that I wanted to be a writer. You know what that meant? It meant that I wanted to write poems. The kind that rhyme, particularly anywhere I could play off the idea that "tall" and "fall" rhyme in a pretty good way when you're talking about trees.

When I was in college, that writing dream changed to writing articles for my school newspaper. After college I wrote advertising copy, including jingles for laser hair removal companies. Later on I would write technical copy for a software company. Now I write self-help, nonfiction books. Do you think that in the third grade I would have said that would be what the thirty-eight-year-old me would do? Of course not.

It's not just writers who experience this either, it's folks like Ultimate Fighting Trainers. (Although the two groups are so similar it almost feels redundant talking about both.) John Hackleman is one of the top trainers in the world. For twenty years, he trained Chuck Liddell, one of the most successful UFC fighters in the history of the sport. He contacted me for help one day. I figured it was a question about a choke hold or something (it's all in the forearm, by the way), but that's not what he wanted help with. He wanted me to help him rebrand because his dream was changing. His gym, the Pit, had too hardcore a reputation to attract the new group of clients he wanted to help: kids. In addition to training top fighters, he has a passion to help teach karate to little kids. This is not something he's doing because his original dream wasn't successful. He is at the very top of his field. He just happens to love helping kids and adults learn karate. Why? Because dreams change. Sometimes what drives your Career Do Over might not even be related directly to your work.

I took a job with the Home Depot, not because I felt like that was my calling, but because I wanted to raise my kids near their grandparents. Geography drove that Do Over, not work. Once we were established in Atlanta, I had more margin to start looking for a job that better suited my skills. You will launch your Career Do Over moments for far more reasons than just chasing a passion.

I hope you figure out something broad and loose you want to do with your career, like writing, but don't get stuck trying to get crazy specific. It's going to change, so aim for flexibility, not rigidity.

▪ Be Flexible with Your Definition of Success

Robin O'Bryant wanted to write a book with a big publisher. Every writer dreams of being signed by a publishing house that also printed Hemingway. Even though self-publishing has come a tremendous way in the last ten years and is a great option, it's common for writers to feel like second-class citizens if they go that route. I know I mistakenly did when I self-published two collections of blog posts.

Robin knew how to hustle and spent two years working with a top literary agent but had no success securing a book deal. Countless times editors told her that she simply didn't have a big enough platform for them to publish her book.

Her first reaction was to pout and mourn the death of her

dream. It wasn't just about getting a book out there, it was about getting a book published by someone who had fancy stationery and business cards.

She might have crawled back off into anonymity, voluntarily never writing another book. But her blog readers wouldn't shut up. They kept pestering her over and over again. "When's your book coming out?" they asked in the comments. "How's your book coming?" they tweeted. In those moments, her readers were being amazing boomerang relationships. Every tweet or blog post Robin had written was her sending out a boomerang that came back in this moment in the form of motivational casual friendships.

Robin fought it for as long as she could, but eventually had to give in after she asked herself the question, "Why did I write this book?"

"The answer was simple: because I couldn't NOT write it. I wanted other people to read it because I thought it would help them, validate them, make them laugh out loud in the bed after a long hard day of wrangling kids. I wrote because I wanted to be read and I knew that self-publishing could accomplish my mission."

So, after much wrestling with herself and deciding to be flexible, Robin self-published her book *Ketchup Is a Vegetable: and Other Lies Moms Tell Themselves* in November 2011. She spent the next two years selling the book out of the back of her car, MC Hammer style. She trucked them to conferences and book signings and anywhere else an audience would have her. She went with grit.

In September 2013, *Ketchup* hit the *New York Times, Wall Street Journal* and *USA Today*'s bestseller lists. A month later, she signed a two-book deal with St. Martin's Press.

Does every story turn out like that? Of course not. But every Do Over avoided because of fear fails. You've got a 100 percent success rate of failing if you don't even try. That's what being inflexible with our definition of success comes back to: fear.

We think hustle is swinging for the fences when we get our big moments, but most of the time, like Robin, hustle is just trying.

We try to redefine success.

We try to self-publish.

We try to apply for a job we're overqualified for just to get our foot in the door at a great company.

We try to go back to school when everyone else thinks we're too old.

We try to open a business.

And when we don't succeed at first according to some predetermined definition of success, we don't quit. We get flexible like Robin did. "I can't imagine what would have happened if I'd been too proud to redefine success. My dream came true because I was willing to work hard. When the door slammed shut in my face, I decided I wasn't too proud to hitch up my skirt and crawl through a window."[1]

That's hustle, that's grit, that's flexibility, crawling through a window when the door is slammed shut.

■ Let New Be Different, Not Old

We think that we can launch a Do Over and things will stay the same or return to how they used to be.

They won't. At the heart of a Do Over is change, and at the heart of change is the word "different." It can mean good or bad, wonderful or terrible, depending on the circumstances, but the one word different never means is "same."

Your life will be different when you experience a Do Over and the sooner you accept that with flexibility, the easier things will be.

I saw this reality headed my way a year before this book came out.

When I worked for Dave Ramsey, during my last book launch I had a team of people who created some amazing marketing for me. The live-events team designed a special event in a 1920s theater in Franklin, Tennessee, to launch the presale of the book. Designers created posters and T-shirts and Web sites. They even wrapped a tour bus to carry me to all the events the speaking representative had booked months earlier. Dave blew the book up to millions of people who listen to his radio show. I bet forty different people were actively involved in the launch of my book.

If I went into the launch of Do Over with that same expectation, I would be a moron. It won't be the same. I don't have forty staff members. I don't have a radio show or a fleet of designers.

I do have Penguin, though. They're one of the most successful publishers of all time and have a building full of talented people. They did all right with Mark Twain's books. They've done pretty well with Seth Godin's books. In addition, I do have access to a lot of freelance graphic designers, programmers and influencers via this thing called the Internet. There're also the relationships I've invested in with my Career Savings Account.

The launch of this book was different from the launch of the last one, but different doesn't have to mean worse. It can even mean better if we recognize that new does not mean bad, and if we actually hustle on the new thing we're doing. Letting go of the old is often the first step you have to take if you want to experience a new Do Over.

It's not just authors who deal with this. You see this in the careers of recent college graduates. Your friends who are still in school call you on a Thursday night to go out like you always used to and you opt for bed instead. You're still friends, but now you have to get up at 6 A.M. regularly. You don't get a spring break. You don't have a few hours in the afternoon to talk in the quad. Most of your life is different when you have your first full-time job and if you try to act like you're still in college, you'll probably lose that job.

This also can happen when you change jobs.

Let's pretend you're unhappy at your job. You realize the results you're getting aren't what you wanted and decide to go back and look at your assumptions like Steeve did. In your current job you're miserable. It's not work you enjoy, you're not that skilled at it and cobras are constantly biting you. Understanding that you don't have to quit your job to launch a Career Do Over, you decide to apply for another position within the company. It fits your natural skill set much better. You decide to leave the old position and accept the new position.

But, six months in, you realize the new job isn't what you thought it would be. It's not that you're impatient or a job hopper, it's just not the job you were promised. In that moment, you will be tempted to look back longingly on the old job. You will see the failure at the new job as evidence that you shouldn't have left the old one. In that moment you will forget all the kindness we said hustle required. You'll beat yourself up twice: once for leaving the old job and once for starting the new one. You'll believe that the failure of the new one proves the failure of your decision to leave the last one.

It doesn't. They are two distinct decisions. Making the decision to leave the old job cannot be judged as incorrect just because the new job doesn't work out any more than you would judge your last boyfriend based on the qualities of your new boyfriend. If the last guy was verbally abusive and you made a decision to leave him, that the new guy is lazy doesn't mean you shouldn't have left the last guy. He's still verbally abusive. The laziness of the new guy hasn't changed that. But we love to idealize our past when our present doesn't meet our expectations.

Don't. When you made the decision to make a Career Jump or choose to do something about a Career Ceiling, that decision ended the moment you executed it. What happens going forward won't change the correctness of that decision.

Be flexible. Doing something new always requires flexibility. It won't be the same as the old thing. It can't. The old is old and the new is new.

They're different and always will be.

■ Have Fun Storming the Castle

No one has fun anymore.

We either think it's for little kids or we think it's for later.

We're completely fine with kids playing and having recess and

being silly. But at some point, it's time to grow up. This is the real world we're talking about. Fun doesn't have a place and it certainly doesn't have a good return on investment.

Or, we think fun is for later. That it's an activity strictly for the retired. We dream of someday having money and freedom and fun. We do the horrible trade with a job we don't love, fifty weeks of drudgery and misery for two weeks of vacation, predicated on the hope that at the end of it all we'll get it back. A neighbor ruined that idea for me, though, one afternoon.

He got in an accident at work. He had thirty years of experience selling tractors and one day during a demonstration, one crashed, ruining his back. In less than a second, his entire life changed.

Swinging a golf club in our backyard, he said, "I haven't played golf in ten years. That's the problem, you think you're going to do all these things when you retire, but you're old. It's harder."

Will you have a freak tractor accident? I hope not. Will you have a company go under and throw your retirement into a tailspin? Maybe not. Will you have a negative Do Over moment that catches you off guard at some point in your life though? You will.

Postponing fun is a bad plan.

We need to have some now, because we might not get to later, but more important, we need to have some fun because it will help us stay flexible and keep us from getting stuck.

Fun for fun's sake is one of the best ways to prevent yourself from getting stuck again. Welcome to an additional tension of hustle. You need to hustle on your Grit List for the necessity skills we talked about earlier and then hustle on your sense of fun for the curiosity skills.

David Drobny knows about fun. He also knows a lot about squall lines and low-pressure storm systems. He tweets about both a lot as the self-appointed Nashville Severe Weather guy or @NashSevereWx. In December 2011, he realized he thought weather forecasting was fun.

So he started tweeting out weather tips for two very specific counties in Middle Tennessee. He doesn't cover the whole state, but if you live in Williamson County, he'll give you the most specific weather forecasts you've ever seen. He tweets things like, "If you're in the pool in the Fieldstone Farm neighborhood, better get out in the next six minutes, there are thunderstorms coming your way."

In addition to tweeting, he also has access to the National Weather Service Chat system, which is reserved for media and emergency management. They didn't want to give him access at first, but David has grit. He kept showing up at the headquarters petitioning them for approval, asking them to see him as "media" until they relented.

During some storms he'll even hit Twitter's daily limit, he tweets so many times. Those are the days he asks his admin to hold all his calls for a few hours, it's about to get fun. Weather graphs, radar models, snow forecasts. David shares it all.

In the years since he's started he's built up an audience of thirty-five thousand followers and received a lot of attention from the National Weather Service as they figure out social media. How much money has he made from doing this? None. That's not the point. He's a successful lawyer. He's not doing this to monetize it. He's just doing it because he likes doing it. It's fun, as evidenced when in the middle of storms he breaks the tension with tweets like, "We don't think that's a tornado but it's being watched like anyone who may want to take my daughter on a date."

The other benefit of fun is that it tends to prevent burnout. My wife, Jenny, is not worried that I won't hustle hard enough on my Do Over, she is worried that I will work too hard. When you hustle and grind and focus, it's easy to become a workaholic. It's easy to keep your head down and look up one day and realize you haven't had fun in a long time.

Fun breaks that cycle, though, because it doesn't have an

easy-to-calculate value. It seems a little foolish even. But fun doesn't necessarily need a purpose. Fun doesn't have to move you forward. If someone asks you why you did something, "Because it was fun" is a complete answer. And kids are willing to answer that way more than we are, aren't they? What purpose does drawing a big rainbow in the driveway have, other than fun? Kids realize that fun sometimes isn't enough of a reason for us adults.

My eight-year-old asked if she and her sister could have a water balloon fight. They didn't give us a reason, other than that their faces said it would be fun. My wife and I said, "Not today."

Thirty minutes later, McRae came back in the house and asked again, only this time, she had a very adult reason. She said, "Can we fill up some water balloons, not for throwing, but just so we can hold them to help us balance on the slack line outside?" (If you're not familiar with a slack line, it's a flat tightrope you hang between two trees, kind of like a fly trap for hippies.)

I got the sense that she and her sister had been brainstorming reasons an adult would use water balloons, given that fun wasn't enough of one for us.

In the context of your Career Do Over, fun is enough of a reason.

So instead of giving you tasks to make sure you're staying flexible while you're hustling, I want you to ask yourself two questions:

1. Is my Do Over sometimes fun?

2. If not, why?

If you said yes, that's awesome. You found some water balloons in your life. Just make sure it stays there as you continue to hustle. It's also important to understand the difference between "sometimes fun" and "always fun." You can't make always fun your filter for success or you will constantly fail. No Career Do Over is always fun. I love speaking on stage at events. I don't really enjoy traveling.

If I were able to teleport directly to events with my speaking jeans already magically on, I would. That I am aware of, that's not an option.

Though I am trying to gain more awareness to say yes to the right things and no to the wrong things, some degree of business travel will always be part of my career.

Getting home at 1:30 A.M. from a delayed flight isn't particularly fun. Constantly tricking yourself into eating an airport burrito at 10:45 A.M. because no flight ever works with a lunch schedule is not super fun. Lost luggage. Cramped seats. Sad little hotels with sad little coffee machines that spit out dark-brown water. Missing some events with my kids. Business travel is only fun if you've never done it, similar to how people who never grew up around snow think it's always beautiful.

You're going to do a whole lot of things that aren't fun during your Career Do Over in exchange for those results no one else gets. So look for some fun in your hustle, but never think that every part has to be fun. Fun is something you add to your hustle, not a filter by which you select which things to do.

If you answered no and aren't having any fun right now, ask why? You were at some point. No one starts a Career Do Over with the hope that if all succeeds they will be more miserable, doing more work they hate, in more stuck ways.

We all start with fun but tend to lose it along the way, often in the face of hustle.

Is your lack of fun due to clarity? You've hustled and gotten closer to a dream that is different from what you thought it would be? It might be time to choose a different path. Is your lack of fun due to pace? You're hustling so hard right now you don't even have a margin for fun. Maybe you need to open up some time in your schedule that doesn't have any other purpose except "fun." Is your lack of fun because this is a med school season and graduation will be fun, but the grind isn't? Perhaps it's reasonable that the fun levels are low right now, but remember that med school has a graduation date.

Don't be afraid to have fun. You've had enough boring jobs. Your Career Do Over shouldn't be another one.

At times, hustle can slip a bit into perfectionism. You start moving so quickly that you get locked into your plans. That works fine until life doesn't go your way. Which it won't. Today, tomorrow too. The planet has an annoying habit of refusing to bend to our every whim. When it doesn't, don't grind to a halt. Tweak your dream, edit your definition of success, let the new be new and some have fun.

Remember

- Hustle takes flexibility.

- Purpose is often a by-product of hustle, not a prerequisite. Don't wait for a perfect purpose. Use hustle as a way to find the next one.

- Never get locked into a rigid definition of success that prevents growth. Crawl through a window if the door is slammed shut.

- Have fun storming the castle. A well-funded Career Savings Account should increase the joy in your life, not eliminate it in the name of progress.

24

Always Use This to Multiply the Moment

*Let no one be deluded that a knowledge of the path can
substitute for putting one foot in front of the other.*
—MARY CAROLINE RICHARDS

In review, at some point during your career you will:

Hit a Career Ceiling and get stuck, requiring sharp skills to free
yourself.

Lose a job unexpectedly, or need one upon graduating, requiring strong relationships to survive.

Make a Career Jump, requiring solid character to navigate the
chaos that jumps always generate.

And finally, in the case of hustle, you will get a surprise opportunity you didn't see coming, requiring smart hustle to make the
most of it. In moments like that, you'll need awareness to recognize what to do, grit to actually do it and flexibility to respond to
the surprises.

The fun thing about unexpected opportunities is that they are unexpected. You don't see them coming, but since you have more control than you think, you can kick start them sometimes.

When you do, you might end up on Instagram in Spain standing next to Skrillex.

Although that kind of sounds like you will be taking a selfie with a tile cleaner, I assure you that Skrillex is one of the most popular DJs on the planet right now. Ask a street youth, they'll tell you.

Misty Jones was in Spain at 6 A.M. after an all-night party, standing next to Skrillex because she dared to launch a Career Do Over. After more than a decade in a job she only liked and at the age of forty-two, she decided to focus on what she loved doing most in life. Music. She didn't know exactly what that meant, but she had a fuzzy vision and that's all you need sometimes.

She'd applied to a yearlong music program with Berklee College of Music while living in San Antonio, Texas. The program would mean moving to Spain for a year. I met her while she was waiting to find out if she had been accepted. Completing the application was voluntary and very clearly in her control. That was a Career Jump decision. Getting accepted? Nope, she had a lot less control over that.

But she got in.

Time to hustle!

She quit her very good, very stable job.

She moved to Spain.

She posted amazing photos on Instagram from Valencia. Some were adventures she had exploring with friends, but most were of her learning how to produce music. Her Instagram feed was a frenzy of soundboards and concerts and classrooms and finals. Given the opportunity to reinvent her work, she worked with a tremendous amount of hustle.

At the end of the year, she graduated from the program. She accepted a full-time faculty job at Kent State in Ohio as an assistant professor of music. Last fall she started teaching music production classes. Without hustle, she would have stayed right where she was, stuck in Texas, dreaming about music but not doing anything about it. That's the sad truth about decisions: not making one is often the biggest decision you can make.

But Misty made a decision, and when it offered unexpected opportunities, like teaching full time, she hustled to make the most of it. Hustle impacts a lot more than just our unexpected Career Opportunities. Your willingness to hustle when you experience Career Ceilings, Bumps and Jumps dramatically increases the amount of unexpected opportunities you'll get.

They won't all be as big, dramatic or obvious like moving to Spain.

Two months into my last Do Over, a company called 2Gather e-mailed me to see if I wanted to speak at Vanderbilt University. I jumped at the opportunity because it was one of the few colleges in Nashville I hadn't spent any time at.

They said that there should be about sixty people in a small, one-hour gathering I would lead at the Barnes & Noble on campus. On a twenty-degree-Fahrenheit night, I trudged across campus and met the awesome staff that was running the show. Unfortunately, sixty people didn't show up. About seven did.

It was a little awkward too because the speaking area was in the Starbucks portion of the store. Imagine you're a college student or professor who has purchased a pumpkin spice latte on a cold winter's night. You've just tucked into a collection of German poetry while wearing a scarf in a quiet Starbucks. Suddenly, over a microphone you hear someone say, "Let's talk about dreaming!"

A handful of people looked up from their quiet moments with hate in their eyes. They packed up their things and walked to the other side of Barnes & Noble until they were out of earshot, staring at me the entire time.

Awesome!

But I went on with my show anyway, hustling my way through

my speech trying my best for the seven people who were there. You don't get better at a skill like public speaking unless you try hard with a crowd, regardless of whether it's seven or seven thousand people. Later that night a professor from Vanderbilt who just happened to be there grading papers e-mailed me to ask if I would come talk to her seniors. I said yes. Days after my Starbucks debut, I found myself speaking to a classroom of fifty students. After that really fun night I tweeted about what I had done. One of the football coaches from Vanderbilt saw it and asked on Twitter if I would come speak to their team. The team that that year beat Tennessee, Georgia and Florida. The team with the coach who was about to leave Vanderbilt to coach Penn State.

I said yes and gave an hourlong talk to a room full of the largest humans I've ever seen. That was an intimidating experience. When I watch football on TV, there's a part of me that thinks, "I could probably beat up a field goal kicker. I could take a punter." Turns out I am gravely mistaken. Even those guys were massive. After the speech I had dinner with James Franklin, the head coach.

He tweeted that night that "@JonAcuff is a beast!"

There are a lot of words and names that have been applied to me over the years, but I assure you that was the first time any human had referred to me as a beast.

Months later, I talked to one of his assistant coaches about going up to speak at Penn State, which would be great.

Will it happen? I'm not sure, but I know I dramatically increased my chances of speaking at Penn State by saying yes to a small opportunity to speak to seven people.

It wasn't easy, speaking for free to seven people when my stupid ego wanted to tell me I was beyond those kinds of moments in my career. The beauty of hustle is that it helps you turn a small opportunity into a slightly bigger opportunity. You get to grow a small yes into a bigger yes. Difficult moments also tend to clear the herd. As I walked across campus in the cold that first night to speak to less than a dozen people, I couldn't imagine where it would lead. But do I remember clearly thinking, "You know where most authors are right now? At home, having a tea. Probably wearing a Norwegian sweater like they sell at the end of the Disney EPCOT ride Maelstrom." Not me, I was on the grind, hustling my way to a gig that I was going to give my all to, regardless of how many people showed up.

Hustle works those two ways. You hustle hard to stir up more opportunities. And then when you have one, you hustle hard to blow it up as large as it can possibly be.

25

Three Final Words You'll Tell Me Someday Soon

O you who sit over your full cup and do not drink, tell me,
for whom are you still waiting?
—HERMANN HESSE

I wrote this book for four reasons:

I am a fan of you.

I am a fan of work.

I believe you are capable of far more than you think.

I believe work can be far more meaningful than we all think.

It doesn't have to be miserable. We need not dread Monday. Drudgery doesn't have to be the main course served up every week. Whether you chase a dream and go off on your own or decide that grit means staying put and improving your current job, work can be great.

But, and this is a big but because I cannot lie, it's on us.

If we want our jobs to change, we have to change first.

We have to plan and prepare. We have to get out note cards and scribble down new skills we want to learn even if it feels silly at times. We have to have grit when we feel like giving up. We have to seek wise counsel even when people tell us things we might not want to hear. We have to do the slow work of planting long-lasting orchards.

We have to build Career Savings Accounts full of relationships, skills, character and hustle.

We're going to need each of those investments because we're going to experience all four types of career transitions: Ceilings, Bumps, Jumps and Opportunities.

Life would be pretty delightful if we could just pick our favorite career transition and then stay there forever. I don't know anyone who would pick the Bump or the Ceiling, so maybe it would just be a decision between Jump and Opportunity. If you hate surprises as much as I hate when waiters sing happy birthday to you at a restaurant, you'd choose Jump. You'd always know what was going to happen next because your life would be characterized by one voluntary, positive decision after another.

Win.

Win.

Win.

Or if you like surprises, you don't like to know what's coming next but would prefer to be amazed at what happens, you'd choose a life full of unexpected Career Opportunities. Your days would be full of lottery ticket moments, a steady stream of awesome things happening one after another.

But we don't get to pick a transition permanently. It wouldn't be good for us if we could. You wouldn't learn some things you need to learn if all you did was win. The defeats we suffer when we hit ceilings or go through bumps tend to teach us lessons we wouldn't voluntarily learn on our own. And a life spent with a nonstop stream of unplanned opportunities would eventually turn sour. People who win the lottery aren't always the happiest people.

No, life is a series of all four transitions. And Misty, the Spanish conquistador from the hustle section, summarizes this perfectly. During the writing of this book, she wrote me an e-mail as her program in Spain came to a conclusion. As I read it, I saw one of the four transitions burst out in each statement. I wrote down what was really at play with each thing Misty said:

left my job of 13 years to go to grad school. left just about everything I had and everyone I knew to move to a foreign country.

Misty did leave a lot behind, but there's one thing she took with her: her orchard of character. She didn't know anyone in Spain. She didn't have the skills to be a studio engineer yet. She wasn't aware of the hustle that was about to be required of her, but she did have her character. When you jump, your character always jumps with you.

learned how to design sounds from scratch. learned how to be a studio engineer . . . on an Avid System 5 no less . . . (translation . . . a really, really big soundboard. . . .)

Hitting a Career Ceiling, a limitation of some sort, is only a bad thing if you let it be. It can also be the catalyst for learning new skills. That's what Misty did here, quickly realizing she'd come to the edge of her musical ability. She developed new skills to constantly break through every new ceiling this new adventure presented. It's a mistake to think the only ceiling she hit was when she realized she was stuck at her old job.

got invited to play/present at a crazy big electronic music festival in Barcelona in June, a project that kept me busy at all hours.

Developing new skills put Misty in a better position to get unexpected opportunities, like invitations to play at big festivals. Misty did not control the Barcelona festival organizer's decision to invite her to play but when they did, she hustled. She had the grit to believe she had what it took to play the festival. She had the awareness to recognize this as a season of extreme hustle. And she had the flexibility to add this new opportunity to her already busy life.

was blessed by a visit from the Long family, the folks who dared me to move.

Oh, what a perfect word "dare" is. Our friends, our advocates, they don't just encourage us, they dare us. To risk. To navigate Career Bumps. To try. We all need relationships like this when we decide to reinvent our work.

filled out over 20 job applications which has been exciting and terrifying.

One Career Jump leads to another. One ceiling broken through exposes a second that needs the hammer of skills too. New relationships open the door to other new relationships. The year was ending, but Misty's adventure was not, it was just starting. Reinventing your work isn't an event, it's a lifestyle. On to the next chapter!

When we read stories like Misty's, it's easy to assume she had magical abilities, talents and connections we regular people don't have.

But she didn't. All she had was her relationships, skills, character, and hustle. All she had was her Career Savings Account. And when she realized that, she dared to ask a few questions:

Why not me?

Why not now?

Why not here?

Those are simple questions, but if you ask them, they will push you out the door. Maybe not to Spain. Maybe just into your current job with a completely different attitude and ability to see what a good opportunity you already have. Maybe into a season of hustle that encourages you to quit searching for a new job the same old way everyone else does. Maybe into making new relationships or repairing old ones.

There's no telling where your career will go if you dare to ask those questions and reinvent your work. Best of all, with your Career Savings Account, you've got everything you need to begin. So why not you, why not now, why not here?

∎ Three Final Words

A long time ago, while I was getting fired from a job, someone told me I wasn't a writer. They essentially told me I didn't have the skills or hustle to be a writer. They thought I'd never be able to do this.

Years later, Jenny and I walked nervously around our neighborhood waiting for a text from my literary agent indicating that publishers had made a bid on this book.

One text turned into two, two into ten. What was supposed to be a one-day auction stretched into two days.

It was exhausting emotionally and exhilarating all at the same time. In that moment when it ended successfully, I remembered the question from that old foe: "You really think you can do this?"

Someone asked you that too.

You've probably asked yourself that question as well.

Fear loves that question.

On a walk in the woods, on a calm spring day I answered it for myself.

"You really think you can do this?"

"Apparently, I can."

I think that can be your answer too.

A year from now, when you write me an e-mail like Misty's, one full of action and hustle and hope and struggles and fear and all the real mess a Do Over offers, that is what I am going to say about you. Sitting in a small home office in Nashville, I'll open your e-mail. I'll laugh and clap out loud at the adventure you went on that you couldn't possibly predict today.

Do you think you can have a Do Over?

Apparently, you can.

Acknowledgments

Jenny Acuff, for always challenging me to lean into the Do Over moments and showing me how fun adventures can be. McRae and L. E. Acuff, I love you! Mom and Dad, for teaching me what it means to be brave. Jon and Laura Calbert, who believed in me so much they encouraged me to jump even with their daughter and grandchildren along for the ride. Nate Bruns and Grant Jenkins for their constant support. Todd and Angie Smith for always showing up when we needed it the most. Andy Traub for refusing to let me give up.

William Warren with the SketchEffect.com for making this more than just a book with your wonderful illustrations. Curtis Yates, Matt Yates and Mike Salisbury for shepherding this book to completion. Maria Gagliano for shaping the words in this book with your unbelievable editing skills. Rachel Moore, who worked on this project and then dared to chase her own Do Over by joining a dance troupe in New York. Will, Adrian, Margot and the entire team at Penguin! Al and Nita Andrews for sharing their big hearts and big ideas. Reggie Joiner and the entire team at ReThink. Thank you for welcoming me into your family. Terry Mitchell, the amazing coffee genius at Thistle Stop Cafe, for showing me and the city of Nashville what a real Do Over looks like. God, for launching Do Over moments with parties for prodigals like me.

Dreamers & Builders

The font is small on these pages but the impact of these people is not. Without the Dreamers & Builders, an online community that turned into a real community, this book wouldn't exist. A thousand thanks to everyone who launched a boat upon the waves this year.

A. J. Bible, Aaron Hoffman, Abbie Unger, Adam Legg, Adeola Oyelabi, Alan Jackson, Alanna Menke Cathcart, Alex Blythe, Alex Snow, Alexandra Veintidós, Alle McCloskey, Allison Dumas, Allison Fox, Allison Freer, Amanda Leigh Carlson, Amanda Leszinske, Amanda Lipscomb, Amanda McNair, Amanda Shannon, Amanda Workman, Amaris Freier, Amaryah LaBeff, Amber Arbo, Amber Boston, Amy Ables Lawson, Amy J. Campbell, Amy Latta, Amy Pike, Amy Sylvia, Amy Warr, Andrea Hultman, Andrea Lacy, Andrea Ragsdale, Andrea Saffle, Andrew, Andrew Engelbrecht, Andrew Nemmers, Andy Tallman, Angela Sims, Angela Standafer, Angie Buchanan, Angie Wilkinson, Ann Fugleberg, Anna Floit, Anne Gubbins, Anthony W. Carpenter, April Bacon, April Best, April Harrison, April Terry, April Wier, Arona Martin, Ashlea Sigman, Ashley Elsey, Ashley Karlen, Ashley Revely, Ashley Weber, Ashley Webster, Audrey Hildreth Lollis, Barbara, Becca Ludlum, Becca Oursler, Becky Caldwell, Becky Castle Miller, Becky Noffsinger, Becky Sheehan, Belle Cagas, Ben Dempsey, Ben McIntyre, Ben Meredith, Ben Snyder, Benjamin Small, Beth Ranck, Beth Whitney, Bethany Johnson, Bill Ogden, Bill Seybolt, Bill Warrell, Bill Weeks, Billy McGarrity, Bob Brundrett, Bobby Hill, Bobby Pugh, Bonnie Atkins, Bonnie J. Blakeman, Brad Daugherty, Bradley Lutz, Bradley W Gann, Brandi Hignight, Brandi Roberts, Brandon Gradelle Smith, Brandon Kurtz, Brandon Spencer, Brandon Weldy, Brandy Anderson, Brent Comstock, Brian Darby, Brian Gurley, Brian Kirby, Brian Krumme, Brian Mintz, Brianne McGill, Brittany Barbera, Brittany Gulbrandson, Brooke Fradd,

Brooke K. Thorup, Brynn Leigh Shamp, C'Belle Tennimon, Caleb Mathis, Callie Burlin, Cameron Mast, Camilla Kragius, Candice Joy Henthorn, Cara Duncan, Cara Willaert, Carissa Wingate, Carla Musarra-Leonard, Carole Baker, Carolina Quintero, Caroline Parker, Carri Russell, Casey Lewis, Casey Sconyers, Cassey Langston, Cat Knarr, Catherine Rincon, Ceri Webb, Chad Sell, Charis, Charity Ellis, Charles Balan, Charles Johnston, Cheray Smith, Cheree Miller, Cherilyn Wise, Cherisse Redmond, Cheryl Brehm, Chris Blaylock, Chris Dennis, Chris Holmes, Chris Morris, Chris Philhower, Chris Walker, Christa Newell, Christian Womack, Christiana Mayer, Christie Kennedy, Christine Royse Niles, Christine Peterson, Chuck Allen, Cindy Munoz, Claire McLean, Claire Troyer, Clay Shaver, Colleen English, Connie Kottmann, Cori Angelino, Cori Schmaus, Corie Clark, Corrinna Hodges, Craig Harmann, Cris and Annie Thomas, Dale, Dan Eberhard, Dan Niedbalski, Dan Noel, Dane Demchak, Dara Crandall, Dave Burlin, David Bisek, David Bouchard, David Dollar, David Efros, David Gibson, David Hooper, David Lerner, David M. Eldridge, David Mike, David Resseguie, David Stippick, David Yuhas, Dayne Sullivan, Deborah Ballard, Debra Hennesy, Denise Dykstra, Denise Legg, Denisse Warshak, Dennis M. Weldy, Derek Duff, Derek Felch, Derek Wittman, Dewayne Havens, Donna Maukonen, Dustin Brady, Ebonita Sonnetbird, Eliza R. Aluculesei, Elizabeth Farquhar, Elizabeth Maxon, Elora Ramirez, Emily Bedwell, Emily Carlton, Emily Easley, Eric Barron, Eric Pangburn, Eric Swanson, Erin Casey, Erin McKinney, Erin Thompson, Ethan D. Bryan, Fred Polacek, Gary Lee, Gena Groves, Genevieve West, Geoff Allen, George Phillips, Gilbert Rod, Gina Davis, Graham Smith, Gregory Williams, Gwen Beattie, Gwendolyn Downing, Gyula Dargai, Heath Lewis, Heather Anthony, Heather Cloudt, Heather Patterson, Heather Villalta, Hilary Parker, Holly, Holly Brennan, Holly Hrywnak, Isabel Hundt, Isabelle Baker, J. Craig Klope, J. C. Howard, Jaci Bounds, Jacinta J. Hampton, Jackie

McGinnis, Jackson Tejada, Jacque Watkins, Jacquelynn Lott, Jaime Lake, James Meincke, James Sommers, Jamie Lapeyrolerie, Jane Tuttle, Janeen Sorensen, Janet Schmidt, Janis McAdoo, Jason B. Weakley, Jason Hoschouer, Jason Sprague, Jay Reed, Jeff Bevan, Jeff Brown, Jeff Ott, Jeffery Ingram, Jen Moff, Jen Ochej, Jen Stephens, Jen Wilson, Jenn Bass, Jenn Sprinkle, Jenna Benton, Jennifer Chin Baker, Jennifer N. Allen, Jennifer Leigh Allison, Jennifer Haner, Jennifer Jensen, Jennifer Kaufman, Jennifer Land, Jennifer Neel, Jennifer Upton, Jennifer Velasquez, Jennifer Weems, Jennifer Yarbro, Jenny Ditch, Jenny Wuenschel, Jeremy Davis, Jeremy Harper, Jeremy Heersink, Jeremy Jesenovec, Jeremy Rochford, Jeremy Shelton, Jeremy Tallacksen, Jeremy Teran, Jess Kosch, Jessica Curry Jobes, Jessica Garbarino, Jessica Jobes, Jessica Krueger-Sheeks, Jessica Martin, Jessica Meulendyke, Jessica Titchener, Jill Shapkauski, Jim Rudkin, Jim Shields, Jodey Smith, Jodi Baldacci, Jody Ferrell, Jody Maberry, Jody Noland, Joe, Joel Wyse, Jon Carlson, Jon Levesque, Jon Stephens, Jonathan Boles, Jonathan Guenther, Jonathan Jackson, Jonathan Webb, Joni Ryder, Jonnelle Rein, Jordan Campagna, Jordan D. Hogan, Jordyn Schram, Josh Billups, Josh Collins, Josh Greenwell, Josh Hatcher, Josh Willis, Joshua Beck, Joy Haynes, Judith Heaney-McKee, Julene Fleurmond, Julia M. Matson, Julia Mata-Stern, Juliann Rager, Julie DeVisser, Julie Gumm, Julie McLaughlin, Julie Morris, Julie Padilla, Julie Reising, Justin Dearing, Justin Fricke, Kaci Calvaresi, Kandi Hamble, Kara Conaway, Karin Tegeman, Karina Allen, Kate Hinson, Kathleen Patterson, Katie Cline, Katie Gabriele, Katie Hawkins, Katrina Shaw, Kay Helm, Kay Pirrello, Kayla Erickson, Kayla Fullen, Kaylei Ward, Keith Flynn, Kellie Kirkpatrick, Kelly Douglas, Kellye Coleman, Kelsey Humphreys, Kelsey Troyer, Kelsi Fulton, Kendra Tiedemann, Kevin Buchanan, Kevin Cunningham, Kevin Jennings, Kevin Wright, Kim Wright-Ledbetter, Kimberli Nelson, Kimberly Gress, Kimberly Himmel, Kinda Wilson, Kirk Bowman, Kortney Campbell, Kris Sellers, Krissy Barker, Kristal

Woods, Kristen Hoover, Kristen Richardson, Kristin Brinks, Kristin Fleck, Kristin Ingram, Kristina Grum, Kyle, Kyle Crabtree, Kyle J. Britt, Kyle Macon, Kyle Price, Laci Urcioli, Lacy Orser, Laretha Hulse, Laura Calbert, Laura Danella, Laura Gutknecht, Laura Hale, Laura Niemczycki, Laura Warfel, Laura Wilson, Laurel Staples, Lauren Lashley, Lauren Phelps, Lauren Wiley, Lauri Goforth, Leah Carreon, Leigh Dusek, Leigh Ann Sharp, Lena Wright, Leo J. Lampine, Lesa Brackbill, Lesley Thomas, Leslie Beyer, Leslie Clark, Libby Norcross, Linda Goodall, Lindsay Demchak, Lindsay Gann, Lindsay Guenther, Lindsay Laidlaw, Lindsey Hartz, Lindsey Johnson, Lindsey Wiening, Lisa Carol Taylor, Lisa E. Anderson, Lisa Landtroop, Liz Clark, Liz Koenig, Logan Metesh, Lonny Rollins, Lori Danelle Wilson, Lorna Gaffney, Luke Sterling, Malachi O'Brien, Mandi Antley, Mandi Monk, Mariah, Mark Brown, Mark C. Ryan, Mark Napior, Mark Tait, Marnie Brown, Martin Himmel, Marvia Davidson, Mary Ann Rouse, Mary Jo McClelland Mueller, Mary Wiley, MaryEllen Miller, Matt Brier, Matt Comisky, Matt Ham, Matt Hochstetler, Matt Rasberry, Matt Schneider, Matthew Habuda, Matthew Lovell, Matthew Wazbinski, May Bohon, Megan Hall, Megan Lee Webb, Megan Millsap, Megan Wasneechak, Melissa Box, Melissa Gandy, Melissa Gnoza Ogden, Melissa Hawks, Melissa Pittmon, Melissa Thomas, Melissa Wright, Meredith Duke, Meredith Quintana Pavey, Michael Armendariz, Michael Branson, Michael Buckingham, Michael Campbell, Michael Cuestas, Michael C. Hernandez, Michael Lett, Michael Lettner, Michael Ulrich, Michaëla Chevalier, Michele Clark, Michele Tyler-Johnson, Michell Bogner, Michelle Cadarette, Michelle Girard, Michelle Hollingsworth, Michelle LaBelle, Michelle McKinney, Michelle Treece, Mikayla Dreyer, Mike Lane, Mike Loomis, Mike Meulstee, Mike Plotnick, Mike Sohn, Mikiala Tennie, Miranda Ochocki, Miriam Lilly, Misha Lentz, Missi Sheehan, Missie Stephens, Misty Hymel, Misty Smith, Molly Fulton, Mona, Monique Walmer, Muriel Brannon, Nancy Brook,

Natasha Bowles, Nate Pruitt, Nathan Borcherdt, Neal Koenig, Neil Brennen, Nic Casey, Nick Carita, Nick Pavlidis, Nick Shelton, Nicole Romero, Nicole Van Velzen, Nikki Lerner, Nischelle Reagan, Otto Rojas, Pam Myracle, Pam Parish, Pam Renner, Pamela Gann, Patti Wilson, Paul Langston, Paul Sohn, Paul W. Taylor, Petrina Turner, Pierre Quinn, Pilar Arsenec, Pira Tritasavit, Polly Vandever, Rachel Bolton, Rachel Mayo, Rachel Zink, Ralph C. Edwards, Randy Kirkpatrick, Randy Langley, Ray Hausler, Rebecca Pettinger, Rebekah Brown, Rebekah Elerick, Rebekah Thomer, Revka Stearns, Rhen Hoehn, Rhonda Tomko, Rick Theule, Ricky Maldonado, Rob Beaudreault, Rob Kaiser, Rodney Eason, Rohit Bastian, Ronald Long, Ronei Harden, Ronne Rock, Roopa Lee, Rosanne Futch, Russell Johnson, Ryan Eller, Ryan Lang, Ryan Westbrooks, Sally Clegg, Sally Rudkin, Sara Noel Henry, Sara O'Rourke, Sara Rose Wilson, Sarah Davis, Sarah Harmeyer, Sarah Anne Hayes, Sarah Hubbell, Sarah Miller, Sarah Parsons, Sarah Rickard, Sarah Roe, Sarah Romain, Sarah Koci Scheilz, Sarah Stanley, Sarra Herring, Savannah Correll, Scott Cuzzo, Scott Harvey, Scott A. Landers, Scott Link, Scott Maderer, Sean Henry, Sean Nisil, Sean Sheehan, Serena Correia, Shana Bresnahan, Shane Roby, Shanna Delap, Shannon Brummer, Shannon Hendrix, Shannon Molloy Schmid, Shannon Tapia, Sharon Brooks, Sharon Goldin, Sharon Mankin, Shaundra Baskin, Shawn Lindstrom, Shayla Eaton, Sheena Mackenzie, Sheila Fiorella, Shelly Tiffin, Sherri Renee Adelman, Sherri Clayborne, Sherri Turnquist, Sheryl Wilcox, Song Flagler, Stephani Halderman, Stephanie Boyd, Stephanie Danbom, Stephanie Floyd, Stephanie Frey, Stephanie German, Stephanie Kilper, Stephanie Lynn Pantages, Stephanie L. Quick, Stephanie Runk, Stephanie Snodgrass, Stetson McElhaney, Steve Curran, Steve Dusek, Steve Goble, Steve Hawkins, Steven Tessler, Stu Gray, Stu Tully, Sue Anne Reed, Sundi Jo Graham, Susan Ward, Susie Finney, Suzi Sullivan, Tabaitha Kaye, Tabitha Westbrook, Tai Stewart, Tamara Taylor, Tamarah West, Tami Romani, Tammy

Fuller, Tammy Helfrich, Tanya Maycock, Tara Fox, Tara Rolstad, Teri Kane, Teri Modisette, Teri Tapia, Terill Jackson, Tiffany Smith, Tim Gallen, Tim Gleason, Tim Weston, Timothy A. Reeder, Tina Bean, Tina Cline, Tina Collins, Tina Hamilton, Tiphanie Uland, Tom Vanderwell, Tovah Atha, Tracy Dusek, Trey Smith, Tricia Wilson, Tymm Hoffman, Valerie Aihe, Valerie Millsapps, Vanessa Barnes, Vanessa Williams, Vicky Cox, Viq Thomasson, Viviana and Ben Estes, Wendy Wright, Weslea McGahee, Whitney DeVos, Whitney Gladden, Whitney Sewell, Whitney Treloar, Will Howell, Will Irish, William Monroe, Win Noren, Zac, Zach Gifford, Zeb Acuff, Zechariah Newman.

Tell Me About Your Do Over!

Blog: Acuff.me

Twitter: @JonAcuff (Tag your tweet with #DoOverBook.)

Facebook: Facebook.com/authorjonacuff

Pinterest: Pinterest.com/jonacuff

Instagram: JonAcuff

Notes

Chapter 1

1. Peter Weber, "Why Most Americans Hate Their Jobs (or Are Just 'Checked Out')," *The Week* (June 25, 2013), http://theweek .com/article/index/246084/why-most-americans-hate-their -jobs-or-are-just-checked-out.
2. Susan P. Joyce, "What 80% of Employers Do Before Inviting You for an Interview," Huffington Post (March 1, 2014), http://www.huffingtonpost.com/susan-p-joyce/job-search -tips_b_4834361.html.

Chapter 2

1. Jules Pieri, "Happiness Equals Reality Minus Expectations," *Inc.* (November 21, 2013), http://www.inc.com/jules-pieri/happiness -equals-reality-minus-expectations.html.

Investment 1

1. Will Wei, "Tony Hsieh: Bad Hires Have Cost Zappos Over $100 Million," *Business Insider* (October 25, 2010), http://www .businessinsider.com/tony-hsieh-making-the-right-hires -2010-10.

Chapter 3

1. Michael Pantalon, *Instant Influence: How to Get Anyone to Do Anything—Fast* (New York: Little, Brown and Company, 2011), Kindle Edition.
2. Patricia Ann Wade, "Do Students Learn Better by Typing on a Keyboard or Writing with a Pen?" *Indiana School of Medicine Newsletter* (April 4, 2013), http://msa.medicine.iu.edu/msa-newsletters/20130404/typing-or-writing.

Chapter 4

1. Kerry Patterson et al., *Change Anything: The New Science of Personal Success* (New York: Hachette Book Group, 2011), 17.

Chapter 6

1. Cal Fussman, "What I've Learned: André 3000," *Esquire* (September 2014), 161.
2. Ibid.

Chapter 8

1. Jason Fell and *Entrepreneur* Staff, "Steve Jobs: An Extraordinary Career," *Entrepreneur,* http://www.entrepreneur.com/article/197538.
2. Scott Barry Koffman, "Turning Adversity into Creative Growth," *Scientific American* (May 6, 2013), http://blogs.scientificamerican.com/beautiful-minds/2013/05/06/turning-adversity-into-creative-growth/.
3. Carolyn Gregoire, "18 Things Highly Creative People Do Differently," Huffington Post (March 3, 2014), http://www.huffingtonpost.com/2014/03/04/creativity-habits_n_4859769.html.

Chapter 9

1. Roy H. Williams, *The Wizard of Ads: Turning Words into Magic and Dreamers into Millionaires* (Austin, TX: Bard Press, 1998).

Chapter 10

1. *Seinfeld*, Season 3, Episode 12, "The Red Dot" (December 11, 1991), directed by Tom Cherones.
2. Sean Woods, "The Last Word," *Men's Journal* (October 2014), 118.

Chapter 11

1. Dara Moskowitz Grumdahl, "Rain Forest to Table," *Sky* (July 2014), 73.
2. Ray B. Williams, "Why Old Habits Die Hard: What Managers Need to Know" *Pyschology Today* (March 2, 2010), http://www.psychologytoday.com/blog/wired-success/201003/why-old-habits-die-hard-what-managers-need-know.
3. Ibid.

Chapter 14

1. NFL Staff, "What Is Average NFL Player's Career Length? Longer Than You Might Think, Commissioner Goodell Says," *NFL Communications* (April 18, 2011), http://nflcommunications.com/2011/04/18/what-is-average-nfl-player's-career-length-longer-than-you-might-think-commissioner-goodell-says/.
2. Heidi Grant Halvorson, *Succeed: How We Can Reach Our Goals with the Nine Things Successful People Do Differently* (New York: Plume, 2012), 43.
3. Jamie Chavez Blog, "Be Regular and Orderly in Your Life so That You May Be Violent and Original in Your Work" (September 15, 2011), http://www.jamiechavez.com/blog/2011/09/be

-regular-and-orderly-in-your-life-so-that-you-may-be-violent
-and-original-in-your-work/.

4. Jacquelyn Smith, "Steve Jobs Always Dressed Exactly the
    Same. Here's Who Else Does," *Forbes* (October 4, 2012), http://
    www.forbes.com/sites/jacquelynsmith/2012/10/05/steve-jobs
    -always-dressed-exactly-the-same-heres-who-else-does/.

5. Michael Lewis, "Obama's Way," *Vanity Fair* (October 2012),
    http://www.vanityfair.com/politics/2012/10/michael-lewis
    -profile-barack-obama.

Chapter 15

1. *The Shawshank Redemption,* Directed by Frank Darabont
    (USA Castle Rock Entertainment, 1994), DVD.

2. Seth Godin, *The Dip: A Little Book That Teaches You When to
    Quit (and When to Stick)* (New York: Portfolio, 2007), 18.

Chapter 17

1. Roy H. Williams, *The Wizard of Ads: Turning Words into Magic
    and Dreamers into Millionaires* (AustinTX: Bard Press, 1998), 172.

2. Ibid.

Chapter 18

1. Marc Maron, "Episode 161—Joe Rogan," WTF with Marc
    Maron Podcast (Thursday, March 31, 2011).

2. Stephen R. Covey, *The 7 Habits of Highly Effective People: Pow-
    erful Lessons in Personal Change* (New York: Simon & Schuster,
    1989), 39.

Chapter 19

1. Drew Guarini, "Fantasy Football Costs Employers Upwards of
    $6.5 Billion, Study Finds" Huffington Post (September 4,

2012), http://www.huffingtonpost.com/2012/09/04/fantasy
-football-costs-employers_n_1855492.html.

Chapter 21

1. Steven Pressfield, *The War of Art: Break Through the Blocks and
    Win Your Inner Creative Battles* (New York: Grand Central Pub-
    lishing, 2003), 79.

Chapter 22

1. Greg McKeown, *Essentialism: The Disciplined Pursuit of Less*
    (New York: Crown Business, 2014), 4–5.

Chapter 23

1. Robin O'Bryant, "Self-Publishing a *New York Times* Best-
    seller." Acuff.me (April 10, 2014), http://acuff.me/2014/04/self
    -publishing-new-york-times-bestseller/.